# HOW TO BECOME A SUCCESSFUL BETA READER BOOK 1

LEARNING THE FUNDAMENTALS OF FICTION

DEDRIE MARIE

Copyright © 2018 Dedrie Marie
All rights reserved
Published by Little Nelson Press
Fort Worth, Texas
Cover Design by Iskon Design, Inc.
New York, New York
Lit-Lucrative is a trademark of Dedrie Marie and is used under license.
www.LittleNelsonPress.com

ISBN: 978-1-7327090-0-3

*For Don and Geneva, who make so much possible.*

**FREE VIDEO TRAINING**

Get the system I use to make my reading habit work for me:

www.DedrieMarie.com/start-beta-reading

Hope to see you there!

*Dedrie Marie*

# CONTENTS

| | |
|---|---|
| *Introduction* | xi |
| *Recap* | xxv |
| *Recommended Reading* | xxvii |

**PART I**

| | |
|---|---|
| 1. Editorial Overview | 5 |
| 2. Genre-Specific Reading | 13 |
| 3. Understanding The Author's Goal | 15 |
| 4. The Jargon | 19 |
| Part I Recap | 55 |
| Part I Recommended Reading | 57 |

**PART II**

| | |
|---|---|
| 5. Creative Writing—The Basics | 61 |
| 6. Genre Conventions | 97 |
| Part II Recap | 133 |
| Part II Recommended Reading | 135 |

**PART III**

| | |
|---|---|
| 7. Beta Reading Etiquette And Tips | 141 |
| 8. Beta Reader Expectations | 145 |
| 9. Helpful Templates And Tools | 149 |
| 10. Final Thoughts | 153 |

| *Part III Recap* | 161 |
| *Part III Recommended Reading* | 163 |
| *About the Author* | 165 |
| *Notes* | 169 |
| *Additional Resources* | 171 |
| *Reviews* | 173 |
| *Disclaimer* | 175 |
| *Start Beta Reading* | 177 |

# HOW TO BECOME A SUCCESSFUL BETA READER BOOK 1

# INTRODUCTION
*The Smartest Folks Read Introductions*

You read in bed, on your break, while working (I won't tell), in transit, on the treadmill, on the pot (um...gettin' a little close for comfort there). You'd just as soon hit up Goodreads than Facebook. Awestruck—it's the only way to explain how you feel about stories and their clever creators. The idea of being part of that creation captivates you. Even more so, it eludes you—I mean, you're no writer, no editor. How can you grow beyond the average consumer without forking over years of study and thousands in tuition? Read on, fellow book junkie.

You absolutely *can* be an integral part of the story creation process with the right help. In fact, collaborative readers (beta readers) are **in demand**, my friend! And I can teach you everything you need to know to get the most fascinating gig in the world—a bibliophile's dream—one you never knew existed.

Look, Amazon should just be called Amazing—straight up. Amazon leads the pack when it comes to innovation. And because of this innovative badassery, it's managed to take the publishing world by the horns and flip it on its head. Gone are the days when an author is forced to submit query after query, waiting and wading through years of rejections from the big publishing houses. Don't get me wrong. This is still an option. Authors still have the choice to take that chance. They may come out on top; or more likely, their arduous work will die a slow death deep in a slush pile on some desk. But it doesn't have to be that way anymore. The answer? Thanks to Amazon—self-publishing.

It's a whole new marketplace out there. This disruption in traditional publishing has allowed thousands upon thousands of writers to publish and distribute their work through Amazon and other platforms.

*So what does that mean for me, Dedrie?*

It means that there are thousands upon thousands of authors needing you to give your pretty lil' two cents so they can put out the best dang book possible; that's what it means! It's called demand for creative feedback, and you could be the target of all that demand...wanted, needed. Sounds good, huh?

*But I don't have a degree in English or writing or editing or publishing*, you say. *How can someone like me—I mean, I work as a* [bank teller, teacher, nurse, mom, florist, machinist, yoga instructor, dog groomer, student, Apple Store genius, hay baler]—what? I'm from small-town Texas; I've baled many a hay bale, honey.

*So how can someone like me help a writer? I mean, my work is nothing remotely related to the writing world. How could someone like me possibly snag an awesome gig like that?*

Beta reading.

*Um, come again?*

Beta reading!

The term "beta" is typically used in the software industry and describes an imperfect or rough release of a product. The beta testers review the product looking for problems and weaknesses before it is launched to the public. It's a nitpickin' nerd's dream job.

I totally picture a room of nerdy gamers sitting in front of a giant screen saying Sheldon Cooper stuff like, "Because you don't have a girlfriend? Good lord, if that becomes a reason not to play Dungeons and Dragons, this game's in serious trouble." I realize if you don't watch *Big Bang Theory*, this may be lost on you...poor soul.

What was I saying? Oh yeah...betas. They are attempting to find every flaw a potential customer might encounter, flaws that would lower the perceived value of the product. And value is everything, right? So best to bust out these flaws before they land in the hands of the public.

In the literary world, these testers are beta *readers*, and they are doing the same: looking for problems and weaknesses in the manuscript. These issues range from structural issues to plot holes to underdeveloped characters to incorrect word usage and contextual flaws, even typos.

> **Note: Beta readers do not edit, copyedit, or proofread the work.**
> **Although, you may find you are drawn to this copyediting/proofreading stuff. If so, maybe you should look into getting some training in that area and add it to your bookish skills. I happen to know someone who can help you out with that. *Wink*.**
> **Um—me. It's me, y'all. Jeez.**
> **Check out the e-course COMMA SUTRA: Proofreading Fiction at www.DedrieMarie.com/lit-u.**

Simply, the author is looking for assistance to improve their writing before it is presented for editing and/or publication. I call this collaborative reading, but the writerly world knows it as beta reading.

The goal of the beta reader is to provide honest, unbiased, useful, and constructive criticism to help the author improve the writing as much as possible before it is placed into the hands of an editor. In a sense, using beta readers can lighten the burden of the editor and, in turn, reduce the financial drain on the writer. Obviously more rounds of professional editing means more rounds of paying the big bucks. Why not help our cherished writers avoid these extra rounds?

Many beta readers are writers themselves and often read on a quid pro quo basis. You know, *I'll read yours if you read mine.* (Somehow that phrase leads people's minds straight into the gutter...tsk, tsk.) Some beta readers read for hobby. Some charge. It's totally preferential. But do you have to be a writer to be able to fulfill this role? Not at all. In fact, most editors are not writers, yet they have the technical wisdom needed to improve the work. It's just about having the knowledge of the fundamentals of creative writing and the skill set to use that knowledge and turn it into feedback.

As a beta reader, you will serve as somewhat of a junior-grade editor or pseudo critique partner with the expectation that you'll throw in your opinions as a reader of the author's genre. You'll point out areas and give feedback but will not actually edit the work or brainstorm as a partner would. And because reading is your passion, the best quality that you most likely already have is that you are a voracious reader—you've covered the groundwork time and time again. But maybe you've not really noticed it on a conscious level. You just need to add a little awareness of that groundwork to your passion and you'll be good to go.

A beta reader's opinion is important to the author in that it is the opinion of a reader, not an editor or writer. There will be an appropriate time for an editor's critique, but that's not what a writer is after when they utilize betas. Authors cherish the opinions of their betas, and they specifically seek the opinions of beta readers who are fans of their genre. But the best ones are the ones that have the perfect balance of being a passionate fan of the genre *and* an understanding of what goes into creating a story within that genre. If an author can find those qualities in a beta—passionate fan, educated enthusiast, articulate reviewer—they'll be forever grateful.

In fact, when I did my research before deciding to write *How to Become a Successful Beta Reader* series, there were two overwhelmingly frequent findings that grounded my decision to pursue teaching this skill: the "you must use betas" recommendations from authors and the "what should I include" question from those looking to beta read. When I searched for resources to answer that question, I came up short—no reference books; just some blog articles and worksheets here and there.

Just about every successful self-publishing author uses betas and recommends them—usually three to five even. Nick Stephenson, the international bestselling author of *Reader Magnets*, a nonfiction series for authors, and the *Leopold Blake Thriller* series says this about beta readers:

> *"There's nothing more powerful than having a group of dedicated readers give you feedback on your work prior to publication."*

Oftentimes that recommendation comes with two caveats: you get what you pay for, and finding a good beta is not easy. (My goal is to change that second caveat.)

Being a genre fan and voracious reader is helpful but doesn't necessarily give you the tools to be an *effective* beta reader. This is why most beta readers offer their "services" free of charge—they don't brandish a strong skill set. Not to say all beta readers are ineffective; however, it is not uncommon for some to offer simplistic, unhelpful, and/or biased feedback such as "Loved it!" or "I didn't like the main character" or "I was bored." This *alone* is neither constructive nor actionable feedback. These areas could rightly need work, and the subjective feedback is crucial, but unless you can articulate some reasons *why* you feel this way, *and* give some actionable suggestions, it's dang-near fruitless.

Also, it can be quite difficult to tell someone that their book needs an overhaul. You must be able to deliver tough information without sounding like a condescending jerk. You must be able to articulate your rationale behind this opinion and give them something to work with. Some folks give praise just to keep the peace. It's like when you're walking around with your skirt stuck up in your nickers and someone tells you how cute you look and stops short of sharing the dreaded news because they're too afraid to say something that might embarrass you. Or you've mingled all night at an important event with a giant bat in the cave and no one had the decency to tell you. *Really?* Walking around with one butt cheek exposed or a booger hanging out of the nose is better than a quick uncomfortable conversation? How does this help? It doesn't. What *would* have helped is if someone had said how stylish your outfit was but that it could use a little "attention" in the back and then kindly guided you to the nearest plant in the corner to inconspicuously attend to the wardrobe malfunction. Or handed you a Kleenex and suggested a quick trip to the ladies' room. Instead, key players avoided you all night or wouldn't take you seriously and you couldn't figure out why.

It's no different with beta reading. How would not being honest in a beta read help the writer? Well, it doesn't, other than momentarily boosting a writer's ego, which could later be obliterated by harsh reader reviews. A beta reader needs to be able to provide *all* feedback, even the negative, so that the writer has the best chance possible to smooth out any snags before the manuscript hits the desktop of an editor, generating editing fees that could have been avoided—or in the hands of the general readership and is met with scathing reviews.

I just recently met Jennifer Egan, Pulitzer Prize winning author of *A Visit From the Goon Squad* at an intimate event at my library. (My library director, who also happens to be my BFF, has the best connections!) Egan was there discussing her latest release, *Manhattan Beach*. She spoke so enthusiastically of her writing process and research techniques—fascinating. We, the audience, were entranced. The questions came at her from every corner of the room, and there were great ones with even greater—and entertaining—answers. But what most stood out to me, and what I most wish to share with you, is the final question of the day.

Egan was asked what has most helped her as a writer. In short, reader feedback. She spoke of her first work that initially went nowhere; she referred to it as a boomerang; and that when she finally sent it to friends and family to read, they suddenly became MIA; that after many missed and avoided phone calls, her mother finally told her the truth. She spoke of the risks of writing in a vacuum:

> *"All I had was the routine of putting words on a page, but what I had lost track of was what makes something interesting to read. And since I wasn't getting any feedback, I had no occasion to realize that I was failing to meet that very basic standard."*

The *art* of beta reading comes in constructing that feedback. But it's impossible to practice an art without knowing the fundamentals of the craft. That's what this book will teach you.

As a reader, you may know that you loved or disliked something, but simply sharing that you liked or disliked the story gets the author nowhere. It would be much more helpful to understand the fundamentals of creative writing and use those to elaborate on your opinions. Didn't really love the story? Why? Just throwing out opinions like "the story didn't work for me" ain't gonna cut it. But if you know the fundamentals of an effective plot progression, you could better identify if what the story is lacking is a proper arc, for example. Your gut tells you something is not right, but how do you sort the specifics and come up with concrete feedback? Something the author can work with? Understanding the craft; that's how. The only way to *effectively* critique anything in life is to know how it's done in the first place. Otherwise, you've solely got subjective opinions to throw around with little to back them, and it's difficult for writers to link those opinions to the technical aspects of improving their story.

I'll teach you about those aspects and elements so that you can easily match your opinions to the fundamentals, giving the author the best chance possible to use your feedback in a constructive way. And it's truly a ton of fun.

This guide is gonna knock your socks off, friend. Here's how:

- You'll feel hella smart when you can identify standard literary elements (or lack thereof) in a manuscript and provide suggestions using said elements to improve the overall work.
- You'll be armed and ready when you can read for authenticity, veracity, and unity of the story.
- You'll make authors think you're a gift from the reading gods when you learn how to read for

proper genre conventions to ensure the story fits the author's intended market (and help them avoid the biggest mistakes possible when launching their book).
- You'll become a literary chameleon when you learn to read with the eyes of a reader, writer, and editor.
- And you'll be thought absolutely charming when authors experience your beta reading etiquette.

It is important to note that this guide was developed with a focus in genre fiction, though I feel it is helpful to have an understanding of the other types of fiction (structured as the novel, not referring to poetry or short stories). Honestly, depending upon which source you find your information, there will be many different definitions of genre, mainstream, commercial, and literary fiction—so much so that it's the topic of much debate. Ask ten different people in the field what the difference is between literary and genre fiction and you'll get a wide variety of responses.

The writing and publishing industries have yet to come up with a standard, across-the-board definition for literary fiction. There are folks that feel fiction isn't true literature or worth reading unless it is literary fiction; that is, fiction in its most artistic form (remember, according to them). Those same people will scoff at genre fiction, labeling it formulaic and inartistic in structure, lacking creativity and skill. On the other hand, you'll find genre fiction lovers that find literary fiction dull and convoluted—written as such for the sole purpose of achieving artistic status among peers.

I personally believe a single work can be both, if we're not stuck on labels here. I believe that genre fiction, which follows a set of reader expectations, can be just as beautifully crafted as the literary work. However, it can just as easily be far too predictable and unoriginal.

Literary fiction can be written so seriously and with such focus on style that its readers find it exceptionally moving, prompting them to explore themes in great depth. I also believe that there are plenty of literary works out there that would bore the socks off just about any reader, all in the name of art. The point is that literary fiction is a free-for-all, operating under its own rules; that is, no rules. Anything goes. The question is: will it be acceptable to readers? Will it alienate itself and be left with a very limited audience? Possibly. And honestly, most literary writers are fine with this.

Genre fiction follows standard conventions and is written for a specific audience, but it's a giant audience. Therefore, it's an excellent starting place for those learning to beta read.

Mainstream fiction is slightly different. It has strong plot lines, attracts wide audiences, and *mostly* adheres to the standard genre conventions but can break the rules a little bit. An example of this would be the story that is heavily rooted in the detective novel genre, but the ending goes against convention: the criminal gets away with it. This type of fiction, I believe, allows the writer to utilize the genre conventions to establish a path while enjoying the creative freedom of breaking some rules. The writer of genre and/or mainstream fiction typically has a strong desire to entertain and grow a loyal readership. As an effective beta reader, you can help this passionate author achieve those desires. But first, you need an understanding of exactly how their desired loyal readership expects to be entertained.

In this guide, I'll teach you the fundamental elements found in the novel—all novels. This means all the types I just mentioned. Because I read vast and wide, which I believe everybody should—from genre to literary—I pull excerpts from all types of fiction to demonstrate my point from time to time in this guide. Just know that while not all examples are genre novels, the elements are the same.

At this point, you may be feeling a tad bit overwhelmed.

*Literary elements? Genre conventions? What? I thought I was just gonna get to read books before everyone else—maybe some of soon-to-be famous authors. This other stuff seems a bit...scary.*

Not to worry! Keep reading and you will find that I've provided you with plenty of information to understand the process and the lingo.

Also, I know it's a tough world out there and we all suffer from time to time with self-doubt and fear, especially when tackling something new. But this is a really fun skill set to learn, and if you follow this guide, you'll have the know-how to do this! To keep you moving in a positive direction, I've included some helpful tips to nudge you to get organized, stay on course, and keep motivated. This guide will be sure to enlighten you just how authors get from *Once Upon a Time* to *The End* so you'll know how to read like a pro!

Now, if I were you, my lil' antennae would have tingled when I read about beta readers working for free, quid pro quo, or a fee. I personally don't work for free. I understand some have an interest in having a hobby that they excel in. I get it. But for those who want to earn from their reading, and with a skill set that authors seek out more often than not, beta reading can be just the ticket. There are plenty of folks who beta for a fee—just Google "beta reading service" and see what pops up.

This book is designed to teach you the fundamental elements of fiction writing so that you have something concrete to reference when beta reading. And it'll give you some questions to consider when reading. But if you find you'd like more in-depth guidance about the act of beta reading and constructing the actual feedback, you can read *How to Become a Successful Beta Reader Book 2: Mastering the Art of Crafting Feedback.* It covers what's needed to get you those irresistible qualities, skills, and practices that all the authors will shout from the rooftops about.

In each of these books, I will also help you keep a pulse on your confidence levels, because having knowledge and skills is just one-half of the equation; you must have the confidence to be able to put those valuable skills to work. I'll give you a tip or two about confidence: walking the walk, and taking control of your new bookish venture. Being the newbie in an unfamiliar world can feel like showing up to the junior high lunch room holding a sad saggy paper sack without a friend in sight. I'll be your friend. I'll guide you until you find your place and voice and confidence to tackle your new beta reading life. (I'm so excited for you already!) And just know that you are not alone in learning this fun stuff. I've got a private Facebook group that I would love to see you in. There you'll find newbie betas just like you (and some with experience and great advice and encouragement to offer), folks who adore fiction and are eager to learn and jump (or slowly ease) into this new and unfamiliar side of the world of books.

So what do ya say?

Look. The captivating world of books needs you like never before. And I'm dedicated to helping book lovers turn their passion for fiction into fascinating "anywhere ya want" careers or side gigs or hobbies...whatever floats your boat. So I think if you're serious about reading with a purpose, a purpose that benefits you, authors, and other readers, then you've found the perfect guide (and gal...that's me!) to set you on the path to a glorious new and exciting adventure. Since you're still reading, I'm gonna assume you're gleefully nodding your head yes now. Yay! And welcome!

**So who is this book for?**

- Readers who are passionate about fiction and want to contribute to that fiction in a real way
- Anyone who feels a deep desire to help authors craft the best stories possible
- Anyone who is interested in learning the basic elements of fiction

**Who is this book not for?**

- Those already knowledgeable of the basic elements of fiction
- Those who felt whooped by all the reading they've done so far in this book
- Those not willing to invest time and effort in their personal education

Before we start, let me tell you about some super sweet bonus materials you'll get with this guide. I'll provide you with helpful templates and resources to use in your beta reading services, such as nondisclosure agreements, questionnaires, self-editing checklists, and project tracking worksheets. I'll list my recommendations for certain tools and services that have helped me with my beta reading business. You'll also find recommended reading that I felt helped me along my journey in learning this skill, as well as some reading that I found encouraging and relevant.

So with that said, let's get this party started!

# RECAP

In this section you have learned

- a beta reader is a someone who reads an author's self-edited and/or professionally edited work and provides effective and actionable feedback on the overall project
- a beta reader can opt to read for free, quid pro quo, or professionally for a fee
- a broad overview of the qualities and skills needed to become an effective and valued beta reader
- and that you've just hit the jackpot for the most fun and fascinating gig ever!

So congratulations!

# RECOMMENDED READING

*On Writing* by Stephen King

I recommend *On Writing* for those who want to write and for anyone wishing to work closely with writers. I find that in order to work well with someone, it helps to have some insight regarding their process for creation, the basic tools of their trade, and just some unique perspective on the challenges they face. Because Mr. King is such a fascinating and successful writer, I thought this would be an enjoyable and laid-back read to get you pumped up about this new world you are about to embark upon! And don't worry. If you're a fraidy cat, this book's not a scary one.

# PART I

~

"But who should be the master? The writer or the reader?"

— Denis Diderot, Jacques le Fataliste

That's an interesting quote; isn't it? What on Earth did he mean? Is this one of those which-came-first philosophic conundrums? The chicken or the egg? While we could spend hours discussing this quote, I believe it is safe to say that a successful book is all that truly matters for an author. Successful, being the key word, is subjective. I get it.

For matters on this point, I'm going to assume that success for a writer means getting their book out there, purchased, and read. Yes, there are those who write strictly for themselves. I'm not talking about them. I'm talking about writers who yearn to be published and read and make a good income doing so. And there's scores of them. Did you know that there are tons of writers who *write to market*? That means they specifically write what their readers want. And let me tell you, they are bankin', like making thousands a month; and they're serving up new books like hotcakes. I'm not talking about these big-name authors with the backing of NYC publishing houses. I'm talking about regular folks who set their minds to become self-publishing badasses. That's who I'm talking about. So let's hash this out.

I said a successful book is all that truly matters, right? But what gets it there? A masterful team? Readers to declare it so? And then what of the team? The team behind a successful novel typically includes the writer, editor, copyeditor, proofreader, formatter, designer, publisher, booksellers—wait. Then, where do readers fall in this mix? Are they not a *part* of the team? Diderot, I imagine, spoke of readers as being only on the receiving end of the equation. But maybe not. He dang sure was a forward-thinking man of his time. As a *beta* reader, you get to be on both sides of the equation. It's a win-win!

∼

### Did You Know?

Denis Diderot was a French philosopher, writer, art critic, and editor. In fact, he is considered one of the most prominent figures in what became known as the Enlightenment. He was the editor-in-chief of *Encylopédie*, one of the greatest efforts to document and organize all human knowledge (which fell victim to his personal propaganda, by the way) and was an influential contributor to literature, challenging the stilted conventions of the time. *Encylopédie*, took him twenty years to complete and consisted of seventeen volumes and eleven books of engravings. Talk about dedication. The work cost him friendships and ultimately his freedom in its writing, as it was officially banned by the government for its philosophical free-thinking voice.

His opinionated writing style resulted in all kinds of personal consequences. He once had his work burned at the orders of the Parliament of Paris; the Catholic Church intervened twice during publication of *Encylopédie*; he spent a stint in prison for attacking the standard morals of the day. The dude definitely caught some hell. Struggling to make ends meet and avoid a life in poverty, Diderot sold his private library to the empress of Russia, Catherine the Great, who made him the personal librarian of the collection until his death.

Interesting, huh?

Now let's check out just how publishing prep goes down for the DIYer; that is, how the self-publishing author gets their manuscript from final draft to publisher-ready.

# ONE
# EDITORIAL OVERVIEW
*Who Knew?*

~

**EDITORIAL STAGES**

I'm going to walk you through, very briefly, the stages of a novel, from final drafts to being publisher-ready. It's important, if you're gonna dance in this ballroom, that you know all the steps. So let's get shakin'.

Writing can be scary business, y'all. A writer endures a rollercoaster of conflicting emotions: excitement and fear, love and pain, patience and impatience, "this is the best book ever" and "someone kill me now." It's like having a split personality at times. And it takes an overwhelming helping of commitment—and the ability to ignore paralyzing self-doubt—before arriving at the destination coined *The End*. Completing a manuscript is a coveted monumental milestone for many writers and one that some are never determined enough to achieve. This *The End* is party-worthy, no doubt. In fact, there's an entire group of folks that take pics of their *The End* page with a well-deserved drink in the shot for all their writerly friends to drool over.

But penning *The End* is just another beginning. It's when a whole new type of work kicks in. It's like when you've hiked and hiked with a hilltop in sight, only to get to the top and find there's another dang hill, except instead of the rolling grassy hills you've just completed, there's craggy rocks to traverse, climb over, and muck up your super cute new hiking boots. The manuscript now must go through a series of edits—some of which will result in multiple rewrites. This ain't exactly easy peasy lemon squeezy for writers.

There are various routes a writer can take toward the goal of publication. They can take their chances with querying the Big Five, hail to the small presses, or take their writing careers totally by the *cajones* and self-publish. For purposes of this guide, I will outline what I believe to be the optimal editing/revision route for an independent author planning to self-publish fiction.

**STEP 1: SELF-EDIT**

Now, we hope the writer is educated on the ins and outs of manuscript submission. (If not, you, as an integral part of their masterful team, can be a source of education on the matter—just another value to offer! Here's a self-editing checklist you can send to anyone in need. Remember, you'll find full links to all these awesome templates and tools in Chapter 9.) It is common for new authors to question whether they can simply utilize the skills of their English teacher friend, a group of beta readers (hopefully unbiased and effective), or another trusted author to serve as their editor. Unfortunately, these well-meaning folks are not professional editors and should not be expected to deliver the results of one. However, it is an excellent practice for writers to glean as much helpful critique as possible before submitting a manuscript to an editor.

A first draft is **not** what should be sent off for editing (or beta reading for that matter). In fact, oftentimes a manuscript will undergo multiple drafts and self-edits before the author feels satisfied that their work is ready for the red pen. Ernest Hemingway was asked about his revision process in an interview. Here's a snippet of that conversation for your reading pleasure:

> **Interviewer:** How much rewriting do you do?
> **Hemingway:** It depends. I rewrote the ending of *Farewell to Arms*, the last page of it, thirty-nine times before I was satisfied.
> **Interviewer:** Was there some technical problem there? What was it that had stumped you?
> **Hemingway:** Getting the words right.
> — Ernest Hemingway, *The Paris Review* Interview, 1956

A writer should work and rework their manuscript until it is as close as they can get it to a finished book. This process should include self-editing, workshopping with other writers, and utilizing beta readers for feedback.

## STEP 2: BETA READ

Many writers want to know how many beta readers they should use. Of course, this depends upon the efficacy of the feedback, but what I have found is that between three and five *effective and consistent* readers are optimal. I've seen some people suggest upwards of twenty and more. I think by this point, it might be called crowdsourcing! Good thing is that this affirms that betas are a wanted breed. Good news for you.

In this process, a beta will read the manuscript and provide feedback touching on areas of strengths and weaknesses. A beta read can occur in various stages of the revision/editorial process and sometimes more than once, but between the self-edit and a developmental edit is the most common time authors tend to reach out to betas.

Typically, a rewrite/revision will occur after a round of beta reading.

**STEP 3: DEVELOPMENTAL EDIT**

In the process of a critique, the editor reviews the manuscript as a whole and provides broad feedback focusing on the plot, structure, style, voice, character development, clarity, consistency, and any other overall areas in need of improvement. If more detailed page-by-page notations are warranted, a developmental edit will be necessary. This is often the stage in which the most substantial rewrites will occur. Think big picture here! It's also a stage where further editing services such as line editing and copyediting are recommended.

> **Note: You may be a literary buff and/or familiar with the lingo of the editorial world, or you may be a mere book junkie but have no clue what I mean by *style* or *structure*. Either way, please know that you will be fully informed of all terminology thrown around in the writing, editing, and publishing world by the time you complete this guide. This book will not teach you the ins and outs of every step of the editing process, as the focus will be on beta reading; but as a part of the publishing industry, it would be of great service to you (and your clients!) to be well-versed in such jargon. We will get to that, I promise!**

Typically, another rewrite is needed after editing; sometimes multiple rounds are warranted.

**STEP 4: LINE EDIT**

A line edit focuses on the prose and its overall effect. Here, the editor may clean up words or sentences; establish rhythm; identify inconsistencies and voice shifts; and/or suggest changes, additions, or deletions to clarify the writer's intended message.

**STEP 5: COPYEDIT**

Without altering the context, this level of editing focuses on grammar, spelling, word usage, style, punctuation, jargon, consistency and continuity, as well as inappropriate figures of speech before the work is set into type and formatted. The overall goal is to ensure the work is easy to read, grammatically correct, consistent, and creditable. Copyediting is considered the first step of the book production process.

**STEP 6: DESIGN**

The cover design should be done by a professional cover designer, being that this is often the number one marketing tool for the book. A lousy cover will never get picked up by a reader. There could be an award-worthy story between those covers, but unless the cover screams, "Pick me up!" no one will ever know. So I tell my authors to ABSOLUTLEY hire a cover designer. Period. (I used Najdan at IskonDesign.com for the covers in this Lit-Lucrative™ series.) A great cover designer knows exactly what cover a reader is expecting for a genre (yes, there are expectations) and can put a creative twist on it to help it stand out among the masses. If a cover looks homemade or unconventional for the genre, it'll tank a book. So, cover designer—a must!

This is also the point when the interior design is completed. An author can invest in a professional here as well (especially if many photographs or other images are included). Or if their skill set allows, they can utilize book design templates (I love TheBookDesigner.com) or design programs (Vellum.pub is a DIY program that is super easy to use) and proceed independently. Interior design, or formatting, is how the text is arranged on the pages; and it can be something no one notices if done properly (this is the goal) or a distraction to the reader if botched (what a sad reason to have a reader give up on a book, y'all).

**STEP 7: PROOFREADING**

This portion of the process happens once there is an actual proof to review; that is, a typeset, formatted, and designed facsimile of a finished product. A proofreader fine-combs the work for any typos, text or formatting errors, and confirms that the work is ready for publication. A proofreader is the last set of eyes and charged with the task of finding *anything* missed during the copyediting process. Some think this a tedious task; I personally love it. Call me crazy, but proofing is my therapy. It's my own brand of Word Find. If you like games like that, or find that errors readily jump off a page at you, or that spotting punctuation and grammar blunders just oddly gives you a sneaky little thrill, you may want to learn to proof as well and turn your knack for spotting errors into **another** Lit-Lucrative™ skill.

In a very tight nutshell, that covers the editorial process of getting a manuscript ready to publish. As you can imagine, it is quite a journey for the author; and like any worthwhile investment, it can be a timely and pricey one. For these two reasons alone, you can see that a writer must place a ton of trust in the process and the people chosen to be a part of it.

If you recall, beta reading occurs mainly in the beginning stages of the editorial process. The author has finished their first drafts and performed a self-edit. They feel they are ready for others to read it and offer up opinions. Typically, an author will ask someone close to them and/or a friend. Very often they will reach out to their peers from their writing groups. *Ideally*, they will have a handful of skilled beta readers and forego sending the manuscript to little brother off at college and the BFF who means well. It is a very tough position to be in—to be a beta reader for a friend or family member. The author needs effective and honest feedback, not sugarcoating, not coddling—and they certainly don't want for all their peeps to vanish, either, when the needed feedback is too icky to share. (Remember that little story I shared about Jennifer Egan?) Therefore, I am dedicated to educating beta readers on how to analyze and return effective feedback. It's a skill that benefits everyone: the author, the beta, the readership. Once a writer has worked with a professional and effective beta reader, a beta that you will soon become, I guarantee they will come back for services time and time again.

## TWO
## GENRE-SPECIFIC READING
*A Tiny Detail with the Biggest Impact*

It is important to establish what genre the author intends the book to be marketed in. This will allow for a focused read with convention expectations at the heart of consideration. (Don't fret. We will discuss these expectations in Chapter 6.) Obviously, the easiest way to get this information is via an author questionnaire. I like to have the author fill out a questionnaire so that I can have a sense of how they feel about their work, what their perspective is on their strengths and weaknesses, what genre they've intended to write in, and most importantly, what story they've intended to tell.

You'd be surprised how often when what someone thinks they've written and what poured out of their fingertips are two different things. This questionnaire gently coaxes out information to paint you a picture of what this book should be or how the author envisions their book: "I'm hoping my romance makes it to the top 100 of the romance category in its first week. I think people will love the twist at the end!" Then when you read the book, you can see where maybe they colored a bit out of the strict romance genre lines, or worse, colored their rainbow in varying shades of gray as "a twist." Romances always, always have happy endings. So this gray "twist" ain't gonna fly with romance readers. Nope. Not. At. All.

For instance, if this were a romance, which is how this author has planned to market it, and the ending had the love interest, say Larry Leprechaun—what? There's someone for everyone, right? Anyways, Larry Leprechaun is found dead beside his pot of gold, which is empty because he was killed and robbed while waiting for Lady Damsel to arrive, well, you'd not really have a romance on your hands. Maybe some other genre with a heavy romantic theme, but a romance? No sirree. Should the author market their book as a romance (without the gal getting her hot leprechaun in the end), that author will be met by some fierce romance connoisseurs who will quickly, and most likely via reviews, share their disappointment with the whole friggin' world. So getting crystal clear with your author about what genre they are planning to market to and write in are vital for the success of the book.

This is where being well-read in a particular genre comes in handy, especially after you've learned about the genre conventions and expectations from readers. You may have been reading mystery and mystery only for your entire life, getting a jump start with good ole Nancy Drew. But sometimes we find ourselves reading for pure entertainment value (which, holy hell, is what it's all about, yeah?) and give little thought to the intricacies of how our favorite sleuths managed to get to *The End*. You'll read a touch differently once you've become your badass beta reading self. But do not worry. You'll still get to read to satisfy the story-devouring beast within you, but on the first round only. When giving it the old beta reading go (the professional read/round two), you'll need to put on a hat of a different color, and you'll need to keep the conventions in the forefront of your mind.

## THREE
## UNDERSTANDING THE AUTHOR'S GOAL
*Why Bust Yer Hump for All the Wrong Reasons?*

～

First things first, you need to understand where this author is in the writing and editing process of the book. Is this truly their first beta read? Have they already gone through a round and made changes? Has the book been through professional editing and they want one last readthrough from a unique perspective, a beta's perspective? Is this book two of a three-book series? Are they thinking they just want a beta's perspective on typos and grammatical errors? All this information is valuable in forming your feedback to the author. It helps you to know where to give the most focus. Obviously, if this is the first read and big rewrites are warranted, you'll not spend too much time pointing out typos and such. That would be a silly waste of time as there will likely be a slew of scenes cut and added. But if the work has been put through the gamut and this is the last read, one final readthrough before pulling the trigger, you'll pay more attention to such things and be sure the author knows the work needs additional proofreading before launching, if that is in fact the case.

As I mentioned before, understanding your author's goals is paramount to helping them write their best book possible. My primary concern in this area starts with genre. If they have a powerful desire to be a mystery writer but don't seem to have a grasp of the conventions, your feedback can guide them toward rewrites to get their work closer to where it needs to be. However, if they love their story but are a tad bit fuzzy on what genre it should be marketed in, then the focus can be on helping them to identify where their work would best fit in the genre categories, subsequently providing them with the best chances for marketing it appropriately and avoiding wasted time and energy on rewrite recommendations.

> Note: When it comes to publishing, the words *genre*, *category*, and *keyword* all have a unique function and don't necessarily adhere to the definition of the terms one might find in a dictionary. Remember, online marketplaces like Amazon are not bookstores, but search engines. So, an author knowing these key elements is vital to having a discoverable book. Here's what each stand for:
>
> Genre: a classification system (able to change with trends over time)
>
> Category: a division within that system that identifies the book as part of a group; the broad terms that describe the book that breaks down into further subcategories; akin to sections in a bookstore; a browse path for a search engine
>
> Keywords: tags that make the work discoverable by readers; they reflect the words customers will type in when searching, narrowing down the focus of the search
>
> The best analogy for understanding categories and keywords is to say that categories are like sections in a library and the keywords are the librarians,

**guiding the readers to the desired books on the shelves located in a specific section.**

While on the topic of genre and understanding the author's goals, it is very important that you communicate whether you are in their target audience. You may beta for many genres, and that's fine. But if you'd just as soon have an ingrown toenail removed than read space military, then you'd better let that space military author know. It's not fair to the author, or yourself frankly, to read something you can't possibly enjoy.

After determining the intended genre, I want to know where they feel their story is a bit wobbly. This can be gathered from the strengths and weaknesses they've supplied within the questionnaire (see Chapter 9). Maybe they feel great about creating a solid plot but are concerned with the main character's arc. Or maybe they feel they've written round characters with great development but worry about nailing the dialogue. While maintaining a close reading for overall strengths and weaknesses and pointing out any areas that need additional attention, you'll need to be sure to keep in mind the author's primary concerns. Be certain to specifically address them, giving the author the peace of mind that you've listened to their concerns with great consideration. You may in fact feel there are other areas that need more help than what they realize, and that's good, that's your job to notice; but if you don't specifically touch on what they've asked of you, you'll likely not get any repeat requests to read for them again, or worse, a poor review of your services among their peers. Yikes!

# FOUR
## THE JARGON
*Talkin' the Talk*

As I mentioned in Chapter 1, there are beta readers who are also writers, there are beta readers who are editors, and there are beta readers who are strictly readers. This guide is geared toward the beta reader who is strictly a reader; that is, someone who loves, loves, loves to read, has no literary background other than enjoying reading, and would like to turn their passion into a fun skill set. With this in mind, I am going to assume that there is a limited knowledge base of literary terminology and the fundamentals of creative writing (novels in particular) as well as the jargon used in the publishing industry. And this is totally cool. I mean, why would you even know this lingo? Or, you may be an English major or work in publishing and know all of this (and are reading this out of curiosity?), but I'm betting most are not. For you freshly interested folks, I got your back!

While it is not necessary to be able to scribble out feedback with the fury and wordsmith powers of an English doctorate or managing editor, it certainly will improve the articulation of your thoughts on the matter to know a word or two specific to the literary and publishing industry.

> "Your character is a little…uh…well, she's kind of like… what's the word? Well, she just needs…something."

Cue author groan. This is one of the reasons beta reading gets a rap as a service that should be free. *That* mess above **should** be free...or banned really. Sounding like a clueless outsider trying to skate your way into the cool cat society ain't gonna cut it. You gotta be able to throw down with a little lingo, know what to say and what others are saying. Not knowing what your author means when they send you a question wondering if their antagonist's diction is believable (get your head out of the gutter; we ain't talking size here) might make your job a little difficult. But if you do understand this terminology, you can address the words their villain uses like a pro. (See, nothing to do with his...member.)

You may very well form quite the steady professional relationship with a writer and find yourself being asked questions about getting published or if you know anything about writing a blurb. Why would they ask a beta something like this? Because it's assumed that you work with other authors. Obviously, you aren't required to know all of this to beta read a book, but it will help in the long run to be able to maintain a professional conversation about such things. Now, I don't really feel all writers will necessarily have a strong literary or publishing terminology base, but it sure would be nice to be able to hold your own in a conversation with one that does. You may find yourself forming relationships with editors as referral sources as well, both to and from. Your services will be taken more seriously if you appear to have a sound understanding of the industry they work in. I mean, you are wanting to have a presence in this editorial world, after all. Makes sense to know the lingo!

So let's start with the basics and some common standards. These definitions or descriptions are my simplistic way of explaining these terms. These are not hard-and-fast published definitions, so don't get all stickler on me. You'll likely find a variation of each word depending on where you look. Also, please know that I fully realize how arid and dull a glossary of terms can be. You read for fun; I get it. I don't want to induce snoring or page turning; so I've made every attempt to make this glossary a less-than-mind-numbing read. How's that for salesmanship, folks?

**I'll start with the biggies:**

**Creative writing** is writing that uses the imagination to compose the form and content of a work. This literary term describes a type of writing as opposed to a value judgment such as "that was some impressive imaginative writing." Fiction, in essence, is creative writing (even if not written very creatively).

A **novel** is a work of written fiction. The length varies anywhere from 50,000 to 300,000 words. In the car world, this would be from the Impala on up to a Hummer Limousine ready to haul all the cool cats to the big par-tay.

A **novella** is a work of fiction that is like the Sedan of books. Not quite big enough to hang with the Impala; not quite tiny enough to play with the Mini Cooper.

A **short story** is 1,000 to 30,000 words. Here's your Mini, y'all. Ain't it cute!

A typical manuscript **page** has approximately 250 words.

A **manuscript** is a written or typed document; the original version before publication. Some people like to feel all fancy with this word.

*Curious Kate: "You're a writer? Really? What have you written? Anything I would know?"*
*Fancypants Frank: "Well, my current manuscript is in its developmental phases at the moment..."*

Just call it your book, brah.

**Fiction** is invented prose that causes sleepless nights for those writing (what the hell was I thinking?) and sleepless nights for those who suffer from *justonemorechapteritis*. It's when the beauty of one's imagination fills the pages that bring comfort, excitement, thrill, and pseudo lovers to bibliophiles the world over. Oh, and fiction is usually long and complex and deals with human experiences.

**Prose** is the ordinary language we speak (as opposed to poetry) in the written form. It's sentences and paragraphs, not stanzas.

**Genre** means classification; a broad subdivision of literature. Don't get too terribly hung up on this definition as you will find that all kinds of folks have all kinds of definitions for genre. So here's what I'm going with. There are many genres of writing. Fiction is a genre with many subgenres or categories. The following is a list of fiction categories and subcategories (not comprehensive) as structured by Amazon:

**Literary & Fiction**
Absurdist • Animals • Biographical • Coming-of-Age • Epistolary • Family Life • Family Saga • Genre Fiction • Gothic • Historical • Holidays • Horror • LGBT • Mashups • Medical • Metaphysical & Visionary • Political • Religious & Inspirational • Satire • Sea Stories • Small Town & Rural • Sports • TV, Movie, Video Game Adaptations • Urban Life • War • Westerns

**Mystery, Suspense, & Thriller**
African-American • Amateur Sleuths • Anthologies • British Detectives • Cozy • Hard-Boiled • Historical • International Mystery & Crime • Police Procedurals • Private Investigators • Reference • Supernatural • Women Sleuths • Crime • Financial • Historical • Legal • Medical • Military • Psychological Thrillers • Spies & Politics • Supernatural • Suspense • Technothrillers

**Romance**
Action & Adventure • African-American • Anthologies • Clean & Wholesome • Contemporary • Erotica • Fantasy • Gothic • Historical • Holidays • Inspirational • LGBT • Military • Multicultural • New Adult & College • Paranormal • Regency • Romantic Comedy • Romantic Suspense • Science Fiction • Sports • Time Travel • Vampires • Werewolves & Shifters • Western

**Science Fiction & Fantasy**
Action & Adventure • Alternate History • Anthologies • Arthurian • Coming-of-Age • Dark • Dragons & Mythical

Creatures • Epic • Gaslamp • Historical • History & Criticism • Humorous • Magical Realism • Military • Myths & Legends • New Adult & College • Paranormal & Urban • Romantic • Superheroes • Sword & Sorcery • Alien Invasion • Colonization • Cyberpunk • Dystopian • Exploration • First Contact • Galactic Empire • Genetic Engineering • Hard Science Fiction • Postapocalyptic • Short Stories • Space Opera • Steampunk • Time Travel

**Teen & Young Adult** have their own full set of subcategories that overlap with many of the above.

The term **abstract** can be used as both a noun and adjective. As a noun, it means basically an outline of the work. As an adjective, it refers to something general and theoretical, something that cannot be described with any of our human senses...unless you're an oracle or something.

**Absurd** means illogical or senseless and can be used artistically to achieve a specific effect. Sometimes authors get all philosophical and dive deep into the absurd...*what are we even here for?*

**Action** are events that occur and are presented through narrative.

An **advance** is money that a publisher pays a writer in anticipation of a completed work. They typically pay in installments: one upon signing and one upon a satisfactory manuscript. Self-publishers don't get any type of advance, but they get to keep the majority of the moolah.

**Adventure** usually refers to books that are all about the fun and events and skimp a bit on theme.

An **agent** is the liaison between the publisher and the writer, the friggin' gatekeeper to publishers (traditional). They work to find placement of the manuscript for the writer taking a fee from the advance and royalties.

An **allegory** is a story that can be interpreted to reveal a hidden meaning. If you've ever read *Animal Farm* by George Orwell, you know that his creation of how life was played out on the farm is representative of the political events of Russia and Communism. In Dr. Seuss's *The Lorax*, the children's tale is entertaining while at the same time serves as straight propaganda against pollution, corporate greed, and excessive consumerism. Allegory = tricksies.

**Ambiguity** refers to having more than one meaning. This can be used on purpose, providing greater depth and meaning (and hella badass book club discussions); it can be accidental, adding vagueness or confusion for the reader (um, *what in tarnation* did I just read?).

**Anachronism** is the act of placing material, events, customs, etc., in the wrong time period or chronological time.

*News of the Black Death swiftly traveled and left London in a state of panic and chaos. People lay dead and dying in the streets, trampled by the petrified. Gerard looked at his wife, beautiful yet decaying before his very eyes, her fingers black with death, neck covered with the tale-tell boils.*

*"Go," she whispered, "Go be with our son."*

*In his moment of pain and fear and disbelief and grief, Gerard kissed his wife on the forehead for the last time*

*"When you find him, please give him this." She handed him her iPod. "Tell him to think of me each time he listens; and that I'll, too, be thinking of him from the heavens."*

Now, this is obviously a bit of an extreme example. But unless you have forgotten your history and the term Black Death did not take you back to the 1300s, a time long before the handy-dandy iPod was invented (or recorded music for that matter!), this passage will not fly.

An **analogy** is a comparison in which one thing is like another thing, usually used to further explain one thing in terms of another. Think *Forrest Grump*: "Life is like a box of chocolates."

An **anecdote** is a brief narrative, typically used to make a point.

*Gerard nodded. He knew this would be his last time to be with his beloved. "It won't be so bad. Our son and I will see you soon, on the other side. Just like the time we got separated from him during the Peasants' Revolt, my dear, we always found our way back to one another. Now sleep, my angel."*

A tad sappy, but you get the idea. He's using a past experience (the anecdote) to assure her the present experience will turn out okay…even though she's rotting before his eyes.

The **antagonist** is the opponent of the protagonist or main character. Remember Annie Wilkes in Stephen King's *Misery*? Yeah, there's one crazy-ass antagonist for ya.

The **anticlimax** is any action that takes place following the climax or resolution, typically disappointing. *Wamp, wamp, waaaa.*

The **antihero** is one that is not stereotypical of a "hero" and is often an ordinary person. I really wish whomever it was that coined this term would have come up with something else, because "antihero" makes me think of the villain or antagonist. Not the case. It's just that the protagonist or hero happens to be not so hero*ish*, just an ordinary dude or dudette.

**Archetype** is fundamental to the human imagination; it is the age-old model by which we understand human experience; it occurs frequently in literature and is an idea, character, or plot. This bit of mumbo-jumbo is based on a Jung premise that all our current emotions stem from those of our ancestors, in a sense. So basically, when we read something with these archetypes—say, a novel that includes a myth about one's search for his father—we, the readers, will instantly have an overwhelming emotional response from the "collective unconscious." Take that and rewind it back!

The **atmosphere** is the prevailing mood of a work.

**Avant-garde** is nontraditional work that is considered innovative or experimental. Ever read *A Clockwork Orange* by Anthony Burgess? Or watched the film adaptation? This work was so nontraditional, so controversial that it has a history of bannings all over the world. If you've not heard of it, it's a dystopian satirical black comedy.

**Backlist** is a publisher's list of books not published during the current season but still in print.

**Beats** are descriptions of physical action that fall between dialogue. Not to be confused with beatings that a character may receive after saying something offensive.

A **bio** (biography) is a brief writing (sentence or short paragraph) about the writer.

*Dedrie Marie is the author of the Pulitzer Prize winning series The Dale, and the story collection Bits of Life. Her stories have been published in The New Yorker, Harpers, and other literary journals. She is also the creator and founder of Lit-Lucrative™, a school that empowers and educates bibliophiles to turn their passion for fiction into careers. She lives in St. Croix and Fort Worth with her Boston terrier.*

(A girl can dream, right?)

**Black humor** is humor that is rooted in morbidity and negativity. Remember *A Clockwork Orange* I was telling you about? Black humor at its darkest.

A **blog** is an online platform with which to build a readership or following. If you didn't know what a blog was before reading this, please email me at lit-lucrative@dedriemarie.com. I would love to meet the person under the rock. I kid.

A **blurb** is the writing on a dust jacket or cover that promotes that book and author or features testimonials. It is not the surprise goo (what the hell is this?) that moms are known to discover in various places: a shoulder, stuck to their chin, acting as cement holding their doctor's appointment card to their current read-in-progress.

A **byline** is the name of the author appearing with a published work. You would see this more in a magazine or news piece.

**Character** can refer to the traits of a person. It is also the label given to the fictitious people featured in a work. The characters are the cast of the book, the supastars!

**Characterization** is the process of developing characters through various literary devices.

**Chronology** refers to the order of events in time.

A **classic** is a literary work that has endured because of its universal appeal. A notable example is *To Kill a Mockingbird*. That sucker was first released in 1960 and still ranks in the top 100 at Amazon in both the Classics and Suspense categories. Can you imagine? *swoon*

A **cliché** is a word or phrase that is overused and unoriginal, resulting in the loss of intended impact. A book filled with clichés is a bad idea and should be avoided like the plague. The writer needs to learn how to think outside the box or risk the book being rejected, ridiculed, and ending up deader than a doornail. But never fear. Every cloud has a silver lining, and *you*, you badass beta reader, will be like a kid in a candy store, taking the tiger by the tail and whipping it into shape. Once you help the author get rid of the lines that serve as nothing but low-hanging fruit, the two of you will be thick as thieves.

A **cliff-hanger** is a plot device used to ensure the reader will keep burning through the pages in a white-knuckle frenzy to see if the work's main character, who has been cleverly placed in precarious dilemmas or confronted with shocking revelations, gets his arse out safe and sound.

The **climax** is the moment of peak development or maximum intensity in a story, the major turning point, the big O…I mean…

**Closure** is the literary resolution, the final salute, the sense of an ending.

**Coherence** refers to the entire work fitting together and being well connected. On the sentence level, it refers mainly to grammar. You know, like you wouldn't have one sentence all poetic and flowery, Toni Morrison style, and then the next super succinct, as to the likes of Hemingway. Overall, it refers to how well a piece "fits together" from beginning to end.

**Colloquialism** is an informal word or phrase used in ordinary conversation. It is key to believable dialogue.

**Comic relief** is what we all need, right? A break from the heaviness of it all with just a dash of funny.

A **comma splice** is a writing error in which two or more independent clauses are joined with a comma rather than a period (and something that is RAMPANT among writers at large). *Here's a fine example of a comma splice, if you write like this you may as well hop your ass to the top of my punctuation shit list.* I kid. Not all are grammar nerds. That's why the gods gave us fine copy editors and proofreaders, right? (Psst, the period goes between "splice" and "if," and since we're at it, I'd throw a comma in after the prepositional phrase "if you write like this.")

In literature, **conflict** is the juicy goodness of the story. It's just what you think it is: characters or forces in opposition. This can be both internal and external, social, psychological (hell yeah), political. Conflict develops drama and suspense and keeps the readers flippin' those pages.

**Connotation** refers to meaning extended beyond words spoken or written. It's what is being implied.

**Context** is the set of facts or circumstances that surround a work and help to determine and clarify its meaning. If the theme is the guts, context would be the—what? Skin?

**Continuity** is a connected series of events that build a plot. It's like the glue. Without it, ya got no flow.

**Conventions**, when discussing genre, it refers to the agreed expectations of the story structure, style, and subject matter that one would find within each genre.

**Co-publishing** (cooperative publishing) is where the publisher and author split the cost of publishing as well as the profits.

**Copyediting** is editing a manuscript for punctuation, context, and grammar.

**Copyright** is a way to protect an author's work from outside reproduction, publishing, selling, or distributing. It's the brand on the cow's hindquarter letting Next Door Farmer Joe know, *this heifer ain't for you.* No breeding, no selling, no chopping up and divvying out to the co-op.

A **counterpoint** can be used to describe simultaneous development of two or more sets of circumstances that have parallel elements.

A **cover letter** is a brief (but sweat-inducing for the author) letter that accompanies work being sent to an editor or literary agent.

In literature **criticism** refers to the evaluation of a work, not like "Uh, this totally sucks" kind of criticism, but an actual analysis using literary theories, etc.

**Denotation** is the literal meaning of a word, sans connotation or hidden meaning.

**Denouement** is when all is revealed and explained in a work, the outcome, the ah-ha moment.

**Description** is narration that reveals what things are like, such as how they look, smell, taste, feel, and sound. Detail in description can bring a flat story to an all new level when pulled off successfully.

**Dialect** is the way in which language is used in various populations. It encompasses unique characteristics such as phonetics, syntax, morphology, and vocabulary specific to a particular group. Dialect can convey differences in ethnicity, geography, demographics, class, education, and culture. I recently was questioned by my use of the verb "tumped" in my work in progress. I mean, who doesn't know what the hell tumped means? Apparently, folks up North. If you don't know, tumped is Southern for tipped, as in I pushed the upright log until it tumped over onto its side. Then I rolled the dang thang up yonder a bit...for shits and giggles.

**Dialogue** is simply words spoken by characters in a story.

**Diction** refers to the author's chosen words to reflect tone and style. Diction is word choice.

**Didactic** refers to works written to teach or preach. It mostly has a negative connotation attached to the word; so tread lightly if you go describing an author's work this way.

A **double entendre** is a device used to convey a double meaning. Typically, it is used in satirical works. "Marriage is a fine institution, but I'm not ready for an institution." —Mae West

**Empathy**, in literature, refers to when a reader feels what a character feels. This, I believe, is where the true bibliophile is born: out of empathy for our beloved characters. It can also refer to one character expressing or having empathy for another.

**Epigraph** is a quotation at the beginning of a work. It typically is representative of the work's overall theme. That reminds me...let me get on that for this guide.

The **epilogue** is added to a literary work after is has been concluded. It serves to round out the design of the work.

An **epiphany** is a revelation or illuminating discovery, the big ah-ha moment. This happens often for characters caught in a pickle.

An **episode** is a brief event in a longer narrative.

An **epistle** is a formal and literary letter.

**Epistolary** describes novels comprised exclusively of letters. Epistolary novels are stories told through diaries, letters, emails, texts, etc. *Dracula* was one. A contemporary example is *The Perks of Being a Wallflower*.

An **epithet** is a descriptive word added to a name: Dedrie the Facetious. *grin*

An **essay** is a short bit of prose, typically a discussion of some theme or personal thoughts—or possibly even a punishment for acting out in school. "Why I Will Make Wise Choices" by Dedrie Marie.

A **euphemism** is used to purposely obscure the offensive. In the South, when we dole out the old "Well, bless her heart," we aren't actually asking for blessings for the shallow dimwit.

An **exposition** is any definition of explanation of something in writing. Typically, this will come as an interruption of the story to get some background information to the reader.

**Eye dialect** is intentional nonstandard spelling used to reveal more about a character rather than the actual pronunciation of a word and is sometimes used to convey regional or cultural dialectal variations. An example would be using "fella" rather than "fellow." Again, another term that I feel could use some revamping. "Eye dialect" makes me think of some dude giving googly eyes to send a message to the cutie at the end of the bar. This ain't that.

A **fable** is a simple story often making moral points and typically uses animals as characters. Because of this, it fits into the category of fantasy. The fable that comes rushing to my mind to offer as an example is *The Wonderful Wizard of Oz*.

**Fair use** is a provision of the copyright law that says short excerpts from copyrighted works may be used without infringing on the owner's right.

A **fairy tale** is a story involving wonderful and fanciful imaginary and magical characters and is often written (or told, as they sometimes are just stories passed down through the years) for children, though not always. Think "Rapunzel," "The Princess and the Pea," "Hansel and Gretel."

A **fantasy** involves imaginary characters in imaginary settings, i.e., your escape from reality.

**Feminist criticism** is a means of analyzing a work through the lens of the feminist theory: assumes that female writers and readers have a unique view, attitude, value, and concern

—which we totally do, ladies! I'm not one of those "march braless with my picket sign depicting an abstract vagina" kind of gals, but I do strongly believe that women are unique and beautiful and have so much to offer the world through their own brand of passion and creativity. Okay... I'm done. Go ladies! Ahem...now I'm done.

**First person** is the point of view of *I* or *we*. When a book is written in the first person, you are experiencing the events from within the mind of a character. So you get to know their thoughts, feelings, fears, motivations, and opinions about their surroundings and other characters.

A **flashback** is the author's way of illuminating the history of a character or place or event through an interruption of chronological sequence; it is presented as an independent scene often via a memory or reverie.

A **flat character** is one lacking depth and complexity (nothing to do with bra size). Flat is how you would describe a character that is written stereotypically. This is not always a bad thing. It can be useful for carrying out narrative purposes, especially for those characters that do not hold starring roles and the reader doesn't really have to know much about them. They can typically be described using one word or a short phrase: "evil stepmother" or "nosy neighbor." They serve a purpose but do not need their own story arc.

**Folklore** is a body of traditions and legends, typically untrue or unproven, that have been passed down from generation to generation oftentimes from proverbs, myths, work songs, etc. Visit Ireland and you'll get firsthand folklore telling at its finest. One of the best experiences of my life! But if Ireland's not on the radar, you can get some from reading *The Jungle Book* by Rudyard Kipling. It's jam-packed with folklore, and a fun read!

**Foreshadowing** is a literary device used to clue the reader of things to come in a story. Hints, y'all.

**Form** refers to the clearly defined arrangement of the parts in a work, you know, how it's structured. So, like, a sonnet has a traditional form, whereas prose can be highly individualized.

**Format** (in publishing) refers to the physical presentation of a piece, how it looks on the page or e-reader or what have you. There is manuscript format (for consideration by editors and agents) and camera-ready copy or publisher format (refers to the layout seen in a published work).

**Formulas** are often used in writing, such as in detective stories, westerns, romances, and other popular genres. They are conventional ways of developing a story. In this guide, I use the term "conventions" rather than formulas as I expect a writer will spruce them up a bit. It is creative writing after all.

The **front list** is a list of books that are new to the current season. Publishers consider this timeframe to be from the point of publication (woohoo) up to about six months.

**Galleys** are when a work has been typeset but not yet divided into pages. It's the format used (by traditional publishers) for copyediting and proofreading.

A **ghostwriter** is a writer who puts someone else's idea into literary form, not to be confused with a dead dude who continues to write. It is often how writers will "keep the lights on" while plugging away at their own authorpreneurial pursuits.

**Gothic** describes works that contain mysterious, supernatural, and dark elements, such as desolate settings—dungeons, castles, and graveyards—and are often violent, frightening, and strange. Think *Frankenstein*, *The Shining*, *The Shadow of the Wind*.

**Grammar** is the system of rules that defines the structure of a language. It is used to produce and understand sentences, or drive you bat-shit cray-cray if totally botched.

**Hero,** in literature, is the central character, regardless their qualities.

**Historical criticism** refers to the analysis of a work via the historical criticism theory; that is, attempting to understand the work utilizing what is known of the author and historical period in which it was written.

**Historical linguistics** is the study of how languages change over time. This is something to keep in mind should you find yourself beta reading for a novel set in the 1300s. How we speak has most *def* evolved over time and should be considered, especially in the dialogue.

A **historical novel** is one that uses real characters, settings, and events but with the author's discretion as to the accuracy of such events; often purely fictional stories containing real people and events. A contemporary example would be *The Book Thief* by Markus Zusak set in Germany during the times of the Nazi Regime.

**Homographs** are words that are spelled the same but have different meanings and often different pronunciations. The *content* in this beta reading guide is fantastic! I am *content* with all I am learning.

**Homonyms** are words that sound the same and are spelled the same but have different meanings. I *saw* him pick up the *saw* and *saw* that woman in half!

**Homophones** are words that neither share the same meaning or spelling but sound the same. I, *too*, went *to* the same *two* marked graves looking for the clues, but just as Lester told me, none were *to* be found.


A **hook** is a device or aspect of a piece that catches the attention of the reader and draws them in and makes them yearn for more. Hook = key to establishing an interested reader.


**Imagery** is where words summon up mental pictures for the reader. It draws on the senses, all of them: sight, smell, taste, sound, and feeling. Imagery is the trick to giving the reader an experience and showing them rather than just telling them the story.


**Interior monologue** is the interior thoughts of a character. Just as we real live folks have ongoing conversations in our heads all day long (I hope I'm not alone here), so do our lovely characters. Interior monologue is quite helpful in gaining relatability of a character for the reader.


**Irony** is when the expectation and the outcome of a situation don't quite align.


**Jargon** is used to describe the specialized terminology of an activity, trade, or profession. In this case, you are learning the swanky jargon used among professionals in the literary field. Go you!

A **kill fee** is a fee one receives for stalking, kidnapping, and ultimately—ahem, I mean, for work that was completed, either wholly or impartially, and then canceled. An example would be that a writer sends a manuscript to be edited with an expected due date in two weeks. The editor completes half of the work and then receives an email from the author stating he no longer wishes to complete the service. The editor will then charge a kill fee, which is often included in a deposit.

**Metafiction** is literary work that is about fiction itself and its conventions. It takes some serious skill and brass ones to pull it off successfully. For a fitting example, read *Slaughterhouse-Five* by Kurt Vonnegut.

A **metaphor** is a nonliteral comparison of one word or phrase to describe another, a substitution of one idea for another. A metaphor is when you say one thing *is* another. Here's some Southern metaphors, y'all: She's just bein' ugly since she ain't got a pot to piss in. Translation: This woman is financially struggling and therefore lashing out at others in her frustration. But in reality, she's aesthetically acceptable and does, in fact, have one guest bathroom and one master bathroom, both with working toilets.

**Midlist** is the list publishers keep of books not expecting to be best sellers but modest sales.

**Monologue** is speech by one person. So there's no back and forth between characters; you just have one character talking at the other(s).

**Motivation** refers to the conditions that cause the actions of characters. As in life, so do characters have their reasons for their words and actions. Motivations aid character development.

A **myth** is a traditional story (typically of unknown origin) that cannot be logically explained but serves to explain the worldview of a people, a practice, a belief, etc. A contemporary example of a book infused with myth is *American Gods* by Neil Gaiman. Mr. Gaiman basically borrowed myths from one end of the world to the other and folded them within his fantasy novel.

**Narration** is the account of a series of events, the telling of the story. The narrator is the one doing the telling.

**Narrative summary** is the portion of prose that is narrated. In literature, it refers to the part of prose where the author is laying out the story for the reader, excluding dialogue and immediate scenes.

**Net royalty** is a payment received from the publisher after all fees have been paid. Ka-ching!

**Omniscient** point of view means all knowing. The teller of the story (the narrator) assumes the all-knowing perspective and relates thoughts, hidden events, and can jump around in time and place.

A **parody** is a humorous imitation of a person, event, idea, or even a society or culture that is intended to be satirical or critical. Seth Grahame-Smith took Jane Austen's *Pride and Prejudice* and created the parody *Pride and Prejudice and Zombies*.

**Pastoral** describes works dealing with simple and rural life.

Writers often use a **pen name**, or a pseudonym, rather than their legal name. Authors will often write under different names when writing in various genres. A great example is Agatha Mary Clarissa Miller Christie (what a mouthful!) known as simply Agatha Christie (aka Queen of Crime). When she opted to try her hand in romance, she published under the pen name Mary Westmacott.

**Persona** is a narrator created by the author to tell the story, giving distinction between the author's real voice and his/her literary voice.

**Personification** is a literary device used to give human qualities to inanimate objects, animals, or concepts. *The moment her heart surrendered, death collected its prize.* This personifies both the heart and death with the human abilities of surrendering and collecting.

A **platform** encompasses all the efforts made by the author to form a following. This can include a website, blog, speaking engagements, wearing a sandwich board while walking up and down Main Street, and other means of social networking.

**Plot** refers to the arranged series of events in a story.

**POD** means print on demand. This refers to the actual printing portion of the book-making process. You can have books printed in bulk or "on demand" one at a time as needed.

**Point of View** in literature refers to the position or perspective of the narrator, who can either be a participant in a story or just the teller of the story. There are various possible points of view in fiction.

**Proofreading** is close reading and correction of a work's typographical errors.

The **protagonist** is the main character, regardless their qualities (good, bad, etc.). Big Hig is the main character, protagonist, in Peter Heller's *The Dog Stars*.

A **pun** is an amusing play on words. This is *pundoubtedly* a silly example. Ba-dum-bum.


A **query** letter is what an author sends to an agent or editor in an effort to have their work accepted. It is often very brief and includes the author bio and a short synopsis of the work.


**Realism** is an approach to literature depicting ordinary life, regardless how beautiful or retched it is.


**Register** is the manner of writing style adopted for a particular audience. You would write in an informal register when composing a work of fiction; that is; with a degree of casualness. But that novel may contain a letter written by a scientist addressed to the Center for Disease Control containing his research and articulate opinions regarding the inevitable epidemic to come should the government not heed his warning. This letter would be written in a formal register.


**Resolution** is the outcome of the story, a solution to a problem or resolution of conflict.


**Romance** is a genre involving a love story.

A **round character** (as opposed to a flat one) is a fully developed character that is extremely plausible (fully developed as in fully considered by the author, not round or developed physically).

A **run-on sentence** is a writing error in which two or more independent clauses are joined without punctuation.

A **saga** is a long and detailed account about the adventures of an extraordinary character...or what you call the gossip from one teenage girl to another.

**Sarcasm** is the use of irony or harsh remarks or satirical wit typically directed at an individual but can be an overall tone of a work. *Oh, girl, I couldn't pull that off, but look at you!* Translation: Oh, dear god, what on Earth is she wearing?

**Satire** is a literary device or technique that uses irony, humor, wit, and sarcasm to ridicule or scorn an individual, society, or all of mankind.

A **scene** is a clearly defined unit of action that takes place in real time. A work is made up of many, many scenes. Think of scenes like photos in an album. You flip through the album and each picture contributes its own important piece of the overall story, vacation, childhood, what have you. This is what scenes are in a book.

**Science fiction** makes use of scientific materials but remains within the realm of fiction.

**Second-person** point of view is the viewpoint from the narrator and spoken directly to the audience (you).

**Self-publishing** is when the writer is responsible for all aspects of manufacturing, production, and marketing of the work, including the fees, and keeps ***all*** the dollars. I refer to the self-publisher as the authorpreneur because he/she's got to basically run an author empire!

**Sentimentality** refers to an excess of exaggerated emotions; can weaken literary work.

The **setting** is the environment and context (place) in which the story occurs.

A **simile** is a comparison of two unlike things typically used to create a nonliteral image. *That Ginger, she's crazy like a fox.* The easiest way to differentiate between metaphor and simile is that simile uses *like* or *as*.

A **sleuth** is the character in mystery and crime novels that carry out the detective role, though they are not always a professional detective. They are the mystery solver.

The dreaded **slush pile** is the stack of unsolicited or misdirected works sent by authors to agents, editors, and publishers.

**Soliloquy** is speech spoken aloud but representative of the character's thoughts; when a character talks to him/herself.

**Stereotype** refers to simplistic and traditional views, oversimplified and prejudiced attitudes and opinions of something. Think stock characters or actions. Flat characters are often stereotypical.

A **stock character** is one with traditional characteristics but lacking depth or individuality. Think "the evil stepmother" or "the girl next door" or "the mad scientist."

**Stream of consciousness** is a technique used in writing to convey unedited thoughts as they occur. They can appear as incomplete ideas with rough grammar and unique syntax. An excellent example of this is in Toni Morrison's *Beloved* where she uses this technique throughout the book to allow the readers to get to know the spirit of Beloved.

**Structure** is the form or the blueprint of a work or the plan.

**Style**, in literature, can be that of the writing or that of the editing. When speaking of the author's writing style, it refers to the author's employment of writing techniques: vocabulary used, syntax, imagery, figurative language, and the handling of dialogue and point of view. When speaking of editorial style, I am referring to the standards for the writing and design that are typically established by an organization and followed by publishers and editors.

To **suspend disbelief** is to be willing to ignore one's critical faculties and accept, if for a moment, that fiction is fact in an effort to experience the work fully.

**Suspense** is a literary device used to create anticipation, uncertainty, and anxiety of what is to come. It is also a subgenre of fiction.

A **symbol** is a literary device that uses something specific to represent something more abstract. The ring in *The Lord of the Rings* represents ultimate power, not so much a snazzy piece of bling.

A **synopsis** is a summary of a longer work. When sent with a query letter, it is to be approximately a page to a page and a half and single-spaced. (Always check with agents for specific submission guidelines.)

**Syntax** is the way words are organized into phrases and phrases into larger units (the clause). It's the word order.

**Tags** are used in dialogue to indicate a speaker. The words "he said" is a dialogue tag. Some authors get a bit crazy with dialogue tags. "It drives me nuts when they use these distracting dialogue tags too!" Dedrie growled.

The **theme** is the central idea or overall meaning and impact of the story. It's the heart of the matter.

**Third-person** point of view utilizes a narrator with limited or unlimited knowledge: third person limited or third person omniscient; (he, she, they).

**TOC** is the Table of Contents.

**Tone** is a literary term used to define the feel, mood, and attitude reflected in a work and is achieved through stylistic devices such as word choice manipulation or irony or imagery.

**Translation rights** are sold to a foreign agent or publisher.

An **unsolicited manuscript** is one that was not requested by an editor, agent, or publisher and will mostly likely land smack dab in the slush pile.

**Unity** is a literary quality achieved when all the aspects of a work are cohesive and related by a central theme or concept. It's when all the blood, sweat, and tears of the author's work come together in harmony...and then we all join hands and sway side to side—kidding!

**Voice** is a writer's literary personality and is comprised of a combination of literary devices and stylistic techniques.

**Whodunit** is an informal term (that's super fun to say) to describe a suspense or crime story where the reader continues in search of the answer to "Who committed the crime?"

**YA** stands for Young Adult, or if you're unread, it could just mean "you." As in "Ya want to grow some brains? Read a book!"

So there you have it: my version of a glossary. I hope my spin on defining and explaining the terms will resonate and stick with you. If not, I blame you for not having a sense of glossarial adventure. Ha! Glossarial—how's *that* for a bonus word!

## PART I RECAP

In this section you have learned

- an interesting fact about Denis Diderot
- the stages of a fiction novel from draft to publisher-ready and all the opportunities you (beta reader) have to squeeze in between them:

1. Self-Edit
2. Beta Read
3. Manuscript Critique and/or Developmental Edit
4. Line Edit
5. Copy Edit
6. Design
7. Proofread

- the importance of genre clarity and how it impacts the writing of the story, acts as a compass for beta reading, and serves as a browse path for readers looking for their next read
- the importance of understanding the author's goals when utilizing the services of a beta reader
- a bit of lit lingo to beef up the old vocabulary

# PART I RECOMMENDED READING

*Bird by Bird* by Anne Lamott

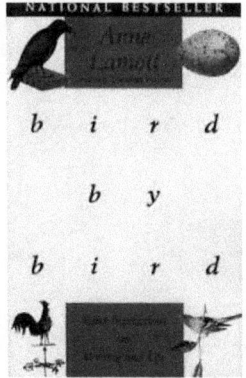

Ms. Lamott beautifully reveals the highs and lows, excitements and terrors of being called to write in *Bird by Bird*. The book is not a how-to but rather a story of how a writer can overcome insecurities to fulfill their passion. I recommend this book to give you some insight as to the vulnerabilities you'll be dealing with (but may not be revealed) when working with authors, which I feel can only assist you in your word choice, tone, and approach when dealing with your clients and prospective clients. If you feel you need a heftier reason to read this, consider it market research. I hope you enjoy. I certainly did!

## PART II

"Prose is architecture, not interior decoration."

— Ernest Hemingway

I love this quote. It's only a tiny snippet of his overall musings about writing, but it really hits home, I think. What he's saying is that writing is serious business. Serious in that it takes time, *much* time, education (whether formally or not), and diligent practice to become an accomplished writer. Part of this learning process involves knowing the building blocks of a story. You wouldn't really expect a builder to just wing it when crafting your home, your shelter, your sanctuary. You'd expect that builder to have a sound knowledge of all the building materials, tools, and techniques needed to carry out the project. This is what this next session will cover so that when you are beta reading for your author, you'll be able to identify these building blocks, or lack thereof, and craft helpful feedback on the matter.

### Did You Know?

Before Hemingway was a published author, he worked as a journalist. While in Switzerland covering the Lausanne Peace Conference, he was asked by an editor to present some of his fiction. Jumping at the possible big break,

Ernest asked his then-wife, Hadley, to pack up his work in Paris and bring it to Switzerland.

The always doting and supportive wife, she packed up everything she could find. Every. Last. Bit. While in route on a train to deliver the goods, Mrs. Hemingway left the suitcase full of Ernest's creative blood, sweat, and tears unattended to go grab a drink...only to find it gone upon her return.

Those unpublished manuscripts have yet to surface to this day. Their fate? No one knows. But could you imagine being the lucky duck who found them stashed away in some attic or something? It'd be like winning the literary lotto!

# FIVE
## CREATIVE WRITING—THE BASICS
*The Most Logical Place to Start, Yes?*

~

Although each genre has its own set of conventions, there is a foundation to all creative writing consisting of these literary elements: theme, setting, time, plot, character, point of view, dialogue, tone, voice, and style. All aesthetically effective works of fiction contain such elements—the building blocks, so to speak—and you need to know them. As the beta reader, it's helpful to be able to identify such elements, or the lack thereof, and determine each element's effectiveness, its contribution to the overall unity of the work. Let's begin with developing an understanding of each of these elements and their functions in the novel.

**THEME**

What is the overall meaning or central idea of the story? Can you easily give an elevator pitch as to the deeper underlying meaning that was spread between the hundreds of pages you've just read? Not what happened in the story, but what it all means? Seems a bit daunting when you first think about it, but stick with me here.

The context covers the surface elements of the story; the theme resides beneath, deeper. What did we say context was again (Chapter 4)? It is the set of facts or circumstances that surround a work and help to determine and clarify its meaning. So this is referring to the setting, plot, and characters—concrete elements that can be described easily with *where*, *when*, *who*, and *how* questions. These contextual elements provide the means to clarify the meaning; that is, the theme. The theme itself illuminates the *reason* for the story having been written at all, the *why* question. It's like describing the difference between what you did in a day versus why you exist at all. The deep stuff.

There is enormous variety in literary themes: the struggle between good and evil, change versus tradition, the circle of life, coming-of-age, everlasting love, own worst enemy, evils of prejudice, fate and free will, individual versus society, injustice, oppression of women—the list goes on and on. And more than one theme can be identified in a work. The point is that there must be some sort of glue that binds the contextual elements and gives rise to the big point the writer is trying to make.

Since we've been on the glorious subject of Mr. Hemingway, I'll use one of his novels as an example. *A Farewell to Arms* is a splendid example of the theme of love and war. Hemingway demonstrates how the two are interlinked: how war puts love in danger; how love can provide solace from the brutalities of war. It also brings home the message that these two married concepts, love and war, are merely temporary.

Sometimes novels have more than one theme. Take for instance George Orwell's *Animal Farm*. Here you'll find two hefty themes: absolute power corrupts and knowledge is power. Let's begin with the first: absolute power corrupts. Mr. Orwell was not one to pass on an opportunity to dole out political messages in his work, and this one is among the strongest. What he's saying is that, though one may rise to power with the best intentions, that power will inevitability lead to personal corruption, which then leads to organizational corruption. In this story, Napoleon rises to a position of power. He initially strives to spread the belief that there should be equality among all animals. That belief morphs over time in his powerful position into the notion that some animals are more equal than others. Orwell is rather illuminating the rise and corruption of Stalin during the Russian Revolution.

The other theme, power is knowledge, refers to the power that the educated have over the naïve and uneducated. In this novel, the failed attempts of the pigs to educate the other animals to read revealed a revelation: that they can simply tell the animals anything, that they could control their education. This message highlights Stalin's control over the uneducated Russian peasants. Without an education, thinking for oneself becomes an impossibility and leads to great vulnerability. (Why we should all be lifelong learners!)

Themes are not always considered when authors begin their stories. Sometimes they reveal themselves as the story comes alive, even for the author. Sometimes they never come to fruition at all, which will require some revisiting of the work. The thing to remember is that theme is important as it is the central idea of the whole shebang. If it's not on point throughout the work, you as the beta reader can bring this fact to the author's attention to help guide her to create a unified story. You can offer suggestions on where to cut and where to highlight and elaborate. The easiest way to use theme as a barometer while beta reading is to ask, does this chapter, paragraph, sentence, or word carry the intended or centralized theme of the story?

## SETTING

The setting is where the action takes place in a story. It's where it all goes down. Every story must have a setting, whether stated or implied, and can serve as a significant role in the work or be almost negligible. Typically, when deemed almost negligible, it will indirectly lend itself to symbolism, tone, or as a backdrop to the more visible and significant experiences in the story.

A setting can be a real location as in an historical novel, an invented world as in a fantasy fiction, within the mind of a character such as in dreams, or a generic location such as an unidentified room, train, bar etc. It is important to identify the significance of the setting in the story. A significant setting, one that is vital to the theme, plot, and characters, will prompt reading for accuracy; that is, assuring the setting is geographically, historically, and contextually on point. A setting that serves more as simply a backdrop to the more focused action will only need to be monitored to make sure unnecessary details don't detract from the reading.

The setting is oftentimes simply thought of as the place of the story, a dot on a map. But setting, if used as a writing tool, can color and shape the people, places, and events of a story. Remembering that the place a story occurs has a collective history among its people will help to hone its relevance.

## TIME

If the setting tells us where the action happened, time tells us when. The time of the story can be straightforward and objective where everything happens chronologically in a specified period, or it can be complicated with jumps, flashbacks, and within a subjective duration. The more complex the time element, the more detailed reading required.

Time, like setting, can also be a real period such as in historical novels, invented and conjectural as in fantasy fictions, subjective to characters as within dream sequences, or generically summarized when stories span extended periods of time.

There are a few elements of time that are important to consider: the overall time frame (during the Renaissance, the Civil War, The Roaring Twenties, the future, for example); distinguishing past from present; the duration of the story; and how transitions are used to bring the reader from one scene to the next.

**CHARACTERS**

The characters are the cast of the production, the stars of the show, the people and animals and invented species and robots that carry out the actions of the story. Characters can be real as in historical novels, created in the likenesses of someone the author knows, or invented as in fantasy fiction. The role of any given character is to carry out actions and say the words necessary for the writer to move the plot along for the reader. Characters can be human or nonhuman, minor players or bigtime players, heroes or villains, sidekicks or stand-ins, likable or hated, well developed (round) or underdeveloped (flat); but each must serve a purpose.

Each character should have a personal motivation that somehow contributes to the overall story, even if only to cause bumps in the road for the main character, or even if to serve as the stereotypical stand-in to allow the author to make a point. A great deal of careful thought and attention should be given to each character in a story. This doesn't mean that every character gets the same amount of spotlight during the story, but it does mean that they all should have considerate thought given during development and serve to advance the story. This can often be achieved by performing character sketches. Not all authors use them, but I highly recommend the practice.

Characters, like real people, have quirks, likes, dislikes, motivations, hang-ups, fears, habits, specific morals, values, and worldviews. And just like in real life, circumstances change who they are as individuals. A battle with an illness may bring about a side of a personality and outlook on life that wasn't visible before. A trip to a foreign country where one bumps into the love of their life will obviously shape him/her as a person. Losing a child to a kidnapper and then fighting for her return and putting one's own life in danger will dang sure muster up some momentous changes in a person. So you see how for a story to work, for a character to be believable, they must grow in some way over time? This is especially true with the main character.

**Note: Growth doesn't necessarily have to mean improve. They just need to show change, an arc.**

As a reader, if you can't point out how a character evolved throughout the story, you may want to mention this to the author. And of course, you can always send them a character sketch template as an added value of your services. A sketch assures an author that her character evolves over time and stays true to himself every step of the way, even if the author's lost track during the freewriting process. It serves as somewhat of a personality blueprint and growth arc of a character that the author can revisit when things get a bit murky.

## PLOT

Plot can be a confusing term for some. It oftentimes gets fuzzied up with the terms "story" and "action." And it's no wonder why. Read up on plot from the likes of Aristotle, Fitzgerald, or Thomashefsky and you'll come away with different opinions on the subject. And really, who am I to question the likes of Aristotle? But for purposes of this guide, let's stick with these general definitions. The story refers to the whole work: a *setting* in which *characters* take *actions*. Actions are the things that the characters do. The plot is the arrangement of these events, the journey.

Let's try it this way: If the story is an account of *what* happens, the actions from beginning to middle to end (the woman killed the guard and fled the basement), the plot encompasses the *how* and the *why* that includes a beginning, middle, and end, but not necessarily told in that very order (the woman whom had been held captive by a sadistic group of men for just under a decade killed the guard and fled the basement). It is organized, shaped, and written in such a way to achieve the writer's desired effect, such as with building suspense. A story is merely a chronological account of a series of events, like a linear timeline. A plot entangles those events in a meaningful way, connects them, and offers up a big payoff for the reader who reads to the end. What happens in your average day is a story of events: get up, shower, eat breakfast, go to work, come home...you get the idea. How interesting is that? Pretty blah, right? Plotting involves taking these events, adding some strong desires, throwing in some challenges, and then carrying the reader along to a satisfying conclusion. It's a chain of cause-and-effects that chug along, building one upon the next until reaching a climax.

There are a few different plot structures one can use as the foundation for their novel, but I believe The Fichtean Curve is the best suited and most popular plot structure for contemporary adult and young adult fiction. It's used over and over by successful authors. Why? Because it works. Here's the lowdown, folks:

- the story hits the ground running with rising action.
- the exposition is sprinkled throughout the first half of the story.
- there are a series of mini crises, like a bunch of baby Fichtean curves that build momentum.
- a climactic conflict occurs about two-thirds of the way through the story.
- the final pages carry out the falling action, allowing characters to tie up any lose ends.

This structure is used so frequently, widely, and successfully by authors because it produces page-turners. Not only do the characters have to keep on their toes, so does the reader.

If you are in the throes of a sci-fi or fantasy novel, or even some horrors, you may keep The Hero's Journey plot structure in mind. It's perfect for imaginative settings with unique character types and adventurous treks. It's basically when a main character is called from the comforts of their homeland to action, an adventure, that is risky but necessary in order to defeat the antagonist against all odds. These journeys often (and should) end with the hero changing and growing. Famous authors have used The Hero's Journey for ages because of its adventurous ability to highlight and symbolize aspects of our own lives. Here are the steps any hero will experience along his/her journey:

- the reader meets the hero in his own world, gets to know him, sees how he lives
- some sort of dissatisfaction is established for the hero
- a call to adventure occurs
- a refusal to that call results from fear of the unknown, failure, worthiness
- the hero finally accepts (usually due to a rise in the stakes) with the help of another
- the crossing some sort of threshold occurs
- the hero gains a better understanding of the new world
- conflict and danger are met along the way
- a decision is made to continue forward, despite the added dangers, solidifying commitment to the mission
- a point of self-reflection occurs, foreshadowing the significance of the major conflict ahead
- coming face to face with the biggie—the major conflict (greatest fear, death, ultimate challenge) —where the hero must pull from the depths of his very being to use his strengths, the lessons learned, and sometimes makes sacrifices to face the big climax
- main character prevails, not without personal sacrifice of some sort
- a reward is obtained and the original problem is solved, but something is still not quite right

- he sets his sights toward home only to be met by the biggest conflict yet: the true climax
- he prevails, finding a truer sense of self as a result
- this character will return home a changed person
- he is met with great welcoming and affirmation that the journey was for great cause

This classic plot structure is sure to deliver an epic story. I mean, just ask Frodo if he got bored along the way!

Okay, what else? How 'bout a little Latin lesson. *In Media Res* is Latin for "into the middle of things." You guessed it. The plot starts in the middle of the story. Take that Fichtean Curve and pull out the second or third crisis. Start there. Now progress forward and throw in some flashbacks and backstory so the reader knows what happened in the true beginning. That's *In Media Res*. Let's break it down a bit better for ya:

- hook the reader by plunging them smack dab in the middle of a crisis (one that chronologically occurs about midway through the story)
- continue forward with a series of further crises and flashbacks
- build until the climax is hit
- progress with the falling action
- continue to sprinkle in some flashbacks and backstory to fill in some blanks
- and finish with a resolution

This type of structure is excellent for suspense, thrillers, and mysteries. It hooks the reader and then takes them along a page-turning rollercoaster of a ride where all along the way puzzle pieces are dropped into place one by one. It makes for a very fun read. Think murder mystery. At the opening of the book, the crime has been committed. There's been a killing. The story then takes you back to the beginning and leads you to the crime and then continues forward as the sleuth (and reader) make their way to the truth.

These are not the only plot structures out there, but I believe these to be the mostly widely used. As with any career, I find it can be beneficial to do a little research on the matter to gain more in-depth understanding. But since you are going to be beta reading for self-publishing authors in this modern day, I'll take a leap of faith and assume that the writers will be using some structures that have a proven track record of success. And if they are not, you will have the knowledge from this guide to offer some suggestions to help them along.

**POINT OF VIEW**

An author writes a story. But it is the narrator who tells that story. And it is with this narrator (sometimes more than one) that point of view comes into play. Think of point of view as perception. Point of view, though easy to define, can be one tricky little booger to keep straight for authors. It can be handled very straightforward and simplistic (keeping the same POV throughout), or it can be creative and complex (with multiple POVs). Let's start with the simple categories. Keep in mind that these categories reflect the grammatical persona of the narrator: first-person, second-person, and third-person point of view.

**First Person**

First-person point of view is told from the *I/we* perspective. That is when a character is telling the story from his/her own perspective and does so using the pronoun *I*. This character shares his/her thoughts and opinions bringing the reader into the intimacy of their mind.

*I walked down to where the blood stained the concrete. Standing so close to what had once been a part of Jack made my stomach churn.*

First-person POV is further broken down into two sub-modes: first person reliable and first person unreliable. These are fairly self-explanatory terms.

First person reliable is when the narrator tells the story as they see it. It may not be 100 percent accurate, as with any subjective account, but it's their best recollection. This narration is the most common mode of first person.

First person unreliable is when the narrator purposefully attempts to deceive the reader as a matter of self-interest. If you've read *Gone Girl*, you know that the story switches back and forth between Nick's account and Amy's account. Both have something to hide and thus deliver unreliable information to the reader.

## Second Person

Second-person point of view is less commonly used in Genre Fiction and uses *you* as a character in the story. The reader is addressed directly, pulling them personally into the story, blending the experiences of the narrator and reader in a universal way.

*You hope that he won't make eye contact with you. You've seen how he can zone in on a newbie, spotlight their inadequacies for all the office to see. So you try to become as small as possible and pray he walks right by you. He stops at your feet. And as if synchronized with his steps, your once pounding heart stops too.*

**Third Person**

Third-person point of view is the most widely used perspective in contemporary genre fiction. It is when the narrator tells the story from an outside perspective but is invisible. They are given a persona by the author, but they are not an actual character in the story. They remain external to the actions and events. This point of view relies on pronouns such as *he*, *she*, and *they*. The third-person point of view is further broken down into subcategories ranging from very limited objective perspective to an omniscient all-knowing perspective. Let's dig a little deeper into the third person and talk about the four conventional subcategories: complete objectivity, limited objectivity, limited omniscience, complete omniscience.

**Complete objectivity** is akin to the fly-on-the-wall perspective. The narrator tells the story from this vantage point only; that is, only what can be seen and heard from this position and at that very moment in time. There's no access to the internal thoughts of characters, no knowledge of past events or circumstances in history. The narrator simply reports what's seen and heard and leaves the expression of opinions and emotions to the characters. This type of narration is most commonly used in screenwriting and plays.

**Limited objectivity** refers to when the narrator tells the story in the third person (again using the he/she/they pronouns) but from the viewpoint of one of the characters in the story, usually the main character (but not always). I'll refer to this character as the target character to avoid any confusion here. This narrator is limited to only the thoughts and emotions of that target character and uses those feelings and thoughts to give the readers impressions of other characters in the story. The narrator can know all the objective information about the target character, such as their past and background, but nothing of any other character unless it is revealed through action, dialogue, or the thoughts of the target character.

*Jackson crept up the stairs as quietly as possible. The old staircase was worse than a guard dog. The popping and squeaking of the ancient wood threatened to reveal his whereabouts to the old man. Jackson's first instinct was to stop and crawl back into the closet. But he knew deep down that he couldn't hide there forever.*

**Complete omniscience** is when the narrator is all knowing. Sometimes it is said that this perspective is a god-like one. The narrator has knowledge of every detail of the story and can choose when and where to dole out the information to the reader. This narrator knows the thoughts, feelings, histories, and futures of all the characters as well as every detail of the time and setting. This narrator can be anywhere, with anybody, at any time. It is truly an omniscient perspective that can hop from the mind of one character to the next, to interpret situations, predict the future, ponder life and death, and offer up some theories and insights into the happenings of the story.

*He was one of those statistics, an anomaly of sorts, born into a family of farmers. He had the brains of a genius, a mathematical wiz; and he let himself settle as a Masco County farmer. The disappointment was not shouldered by his mother alone. His high school math teacher had been equally devastated when he turned down the full ride to university to uphold the family tradition.*

**Limited omniscience** is just a limited version of omniscience. Rather than having full access to all the dang thangs in a story all at once, the narrator is limited to one character's perspective at a time. Think of him like a mind reader that has the power to only read one mind at a time. He may be following a whole group of folks, but he can only give his focus to one person at a time.

What's most important to keep in mind when it comes to point of view is clarity and consistency. The vantage point or perspective needs to be clearly established at the get-go and then remain consistent throughout the work. Even if that perspective jumps around, as in a multi-POV narration, it needs to be clear and purposeful, avoiding accidental shifts in narration at inopportune moments. The goal is unity and consistency.

Point of view can be a brilliant writing technique, but if botched, it can lend to confusion for a reader. Because it takes mastery to effectively pull off a combination of POVs within one work, I typically advise beginning writers to stick with a single POV until they are comfortable with it. As with any skill, master one area, then progress. Trying too much too soon—well, a writer might find she's gone and thrown the horse out in front of her cart. Slow that roll, I say. And this will be something to keep in mind when beta reading. You may find yourself in the position of coaxing an overly ambitious newbie writer down from the high horse of POV complexity. It can be done, and it can be done gracefully.

**DIALOGUE**

Dialogue is my favorite topic. As a writer, dialogue is my strength. Makes sense; I'm pretty much a Chatty Cathy. I love conversation, listening to how people speak, how they convey what they want to say, and how they manipulate with words. Dialogue is a brilliant tool for developing characters (you see how they speak and what interests them; sometimes a character will tell you a story about another character), for delivering sneaky little subplots (maybe a character's words and actions are incongruent, therefore, delivering interesting little mixed and hidden messages), and for revealing actions, both current and in the past.

There is a conventional form for how dialogue is written:

**Spoken material is nestled between quotation marks.**
*"We're livin' high on the hog!" said Billy Bob.*

**A change in speaker initiates a new paragraph.**
*"What do you think about Margaret?" asked Sue Ellen.*
*"I'd say she's blind in one eye and can't see out the other," said Lynn.*

**The first words inside the quotes are capitalized unless it is a continuation of a sentence that has been interrupted.**
*"Well, as soon as his momma showed up," she said, "things went to hell in a hand basket."*

**Dialogue must be preceded by a colon (when the quotation is introduced by an independent clause) or comma (when it is a matter of simply identifying who is speaking).**
*Sara Jean's words were harsh: "I think you're about as dumb as a box of rocks, George."*

*Sara Jean said, "I think you're about as dumb as a box of rocks, George."*

**Closing punctuation varies depending upon the grammatical scenario.**

A comma is used to close a quote if a tag follows.

*"I think you're just splendid," said Lucille.*

A period is used to close a quote if no tag follows.

*She said, "I think you're just splendid."*

Question marks and exclamation points that are a part of the quoted material fall inside the quotation marks. If a tag follows, the first word is lowercase.

*"What do you think this is?" asked Julie.*

*"Beats me!" said Hank.*

**Related descriptive material hangs out in the same paragraph, either before or after the dialogue. If unrelated, it should start a new paragraph.**

*She took one look at him and knew he was the one. Her heart pounded as she mustered up the courage to speak: "So how long are you in town for?" Her vocal chords squeezed tight onto her words, making her voice come across shrill.*

*He grimaced, almost flinching. "Uh, I'll be heading out tonight," he said. He picked up his clothes she had laid out on the counter. "Thanks for taking care of these. Nice meeting you."*

**Dialogue tags inform the reader of who is speaking.**

Tags can be simple.

*I said, he said, she said, Momma said.*

Tags can be varied.

*He chortled, she whispered, I vented.*
Tags can be elaborate.
*Se cried wearily, he shouted viciously.*


**Dialogue can be direct.**
*He said, "I won't go down without a fight."*


**Dialogue can be indirect.**
*He said that he wouldn't go down without a fight.*
(Indirect dialogue is somewhat of a summary or paraphrasing of what was said. It does not take quotation marks.)


**Dialogue uses dialect (the way a language is used by certain groups), diction (word choice), and specialized syntax (sentence structure/order) or idioms (a particular way of speaking or expression of certain groups) to reflect regional characteristics and time periods.**

That came out clear as mud, huh? Let's break it down with an example. I'll use *A Brief History of Seven Killings* by Marlon James.

The first chapter is narrated by Sir Arthur George Jennings.

- He speaks proper English (dialect).
- His word choices (diction) such as "tangent" tell us he's got somewhat of a vocabulary.
- Idioms such as "bloody awful" hint toward a British regionalism.

The second chapter is narrated by Bam-Bam.

- He speaks in Patois (dialect).
- He uses words (diction) such as "chat bad" to mean poor English.
- His sentence structure omits articles and verbs and is reflective of a broken English. In this case, it demonstrates his lack of education as well as the typical speak in the Jamaican ghetto.

*"Me sight a shop that either didn't close or just opening up since is curfew."*

Compare this to Nina Burgess' dialogue.

- She also speaks Patois, but fluctuates back and forth between it and standard (or nonbroken) English. This is used to portray her as educated and wanting out of the Jamaican ghetto life but feeling stuck there at times.
- She too uses some of the same dialect and word choices as Bam-Bam, especially when speaking to people like Bam-Bam.

*"Me pregnant. And is fi him. Him need fi mind him pickney."*

- But as soon as she makes her way to New York, you see the Patois drop away.

*"I wasn't going to spend my life in Maryland, and Arkansas was not going to work out. Besides, a big city is better overall."*

A well-known example of the use of dialect in fiction is in Mark Twain's *Huckleberry Finn*. It's chock-full of regionalisms, country-folk speak, Southern idioms, and so forth. And it's because of these that the reader gets a sense of the characters and how their surroundings and culture shape who they are as a person.

The key to dialogue is keeping it natural, albeit, 1) refined, 2) brief but revealing, and 3) unobtrusive yet purposeful. Those can come across as an oxymoron to natural, I know, but hear me out. To have dialogue be 100 percent realistic would be incredibly boring. So it's gotta be refined. Here's an example of realistic speech:

> *"Hey," she said.*
> *"Hey," Jack said.*
> *"Whatcha up to?" Jane asked.*
> *"Nothin' much. You?" Jack asked.*

You get what I mean, right? Yes, this is how we speak. But we don't need all this riff-raff in the story. Let those characters get to the dang point already!

So what does *brief but revealing* mean? Sometimes, people can get a bit wordy. They can go off on tangents, head out into left field, deliver giant monologues, only to say that they had a crap day. What needs to be included is only what propels the story forward. Ask yourself, "Does this dialogue carry any weight? Does it move the story along?" If not, that means it's not revealing anything; it's just taking up valuable space on a page. Brevity needs to be considered.

Unobtrusive yet purposeful specifically refers to dialogue tags. Tags are meant to alert the reader as to who is doing the talking. That's it. At some point, writers started to get all fluffy and creative with these tags. I'm referring to the elaborate tags that attempt to serve as a descriptive of a thought or statement while stating it. When dialogue tags become so elaborate and fluffy that they catch the attention of the reader, they have effectively stolen the attention from the words being said. Seems pretty counterproductive in my opinion. I say drop the fluff. Drop the adverbs. Stick with he said/she said and let the reader keep the flow going.

And for the record, no one gasps a sentence, smiles a statement, snickers a question. They just don't. You may ask a question and then snicker, but you dang sure can't snicker a question. I mean, try gasping this: "I couldn't believe that he said that to me. What a jerk." Go on. Gasp it.

Okay, you get the point. Let the dialogue speak for itself. If the writer feels the need to tack on adverbs and long descriptives of how he said something, well, maybe the dialogue itself is weak and needs some work. Tags shouldn't do the work of conveying emotion; the dialogue and actions should.

**TONE, VOICE, and STYLE**

If tone is the author's attitude presented in a piece of fiction, voice is her unique writing personality. The two of these together create an author's style. The tone (attitude) can be altered from work to work, just like you can alter your attitude from day to day; but the voice (writing personality) remains consistent.

Just like in life, someone with a keen sense of personal style may present themselves consistently from day to day (personality), with slight alterations (in attitude) depending upon the circumstances.

Consider the Southern Belle. She will be the same woman, have the same morals and beliefs regardless who she is speaking with, and will be easily recognizable as a Southern Belle by her personality, charm, unwavering manners, and use of Southern dialect and idioms. "Well, bless her lil' heart."

However, she alters somewhat her tone or attitude depending upon her circumstances and her audience. If she's at the Governor's mansion for dinner, she may laugh a little quieter, structure her sentences in accordance to the formal affair, and remain a bit conservative. She'll have her pearls draping beautifully above an elegant gown. When this same woman attends the County Fair, she may laugh boisterously while she cheers on her beau who has entered the strong man competition; she may speak in stereotypical idioms reserved for close company only: "Well, I'll be a son of a gun"; she may even give out a whistle and a wave to her beau when he makes eye contact with her from across the way. She'll still have those pearls on, but they'll hang above the denim button-down she's wearing. She handles herself accordingly, adapting her attitude to fit the situation and audience, but her values and personality stay true.

The style of established authors remains consistent, especially within the same genres. The tones vary typically, as each story is unique and therefore the author has a different feeling about the subject, but the voice remains the same. And some authors have such distinct and concrete styles that a reader could identify them by reading their works alone.

The choices a writer makes in point of view, themes, syntax, imagery, how they handle dialogue and punctuation, literary devices such as metaphor and simile, tone of a work—all these things work in harmony to convey a unique writing style. Hemingway had a consistent and distinct writing style, one of unadorned prose. He wrote without fluff. He nailed the point. He mastered dialogue and used it heavily to develop characters rather than having a narrator explain or describe a character. He wrote sparingly and purposefully, each sentence polished to perfection. His background in journalism can easily be recognized as an influence on his unique style, reserving emotion.

Compare this to the writing of Toni Morrison. Her writing style is more complex. She gravitates toward the lyrical, the descriptive analogies. She writes unabashedly and authentically, representing her identity and culture with each work. She writes with intensity and wields metaphor and symbolism heavily in her stories. She manages to write in varied sentence structure, but with consistency.

While both these writers are renowned Nobel Prize winning authors, each have incredibly distinctive writing styles that seem to nestle on opposite ends of the spectrum. What holds true for each is their consistency and authenticity. That's what great writing styles are made of.

So if the tone seems to be the one variable factor in the matter of style, what do we as beta readers need to be considering here? First and foremost, is the tone consistent within the work? Next, what seems to be the reason for the work having been written at all? Who does it appear to be written for? What does the author want the reader to consider or gain? When considering tone in fiction, genre plays a significant role; so what genre is the work? Having clear answers to these questions will lead to identifying the tone, which will then help to clarify the style.

So how can we talk about tone and voice and style with

our authors? Sometimes the hardest part is just articulating this information. When reading, we often get a sense of this tone and voice and style but struggle to describe it. Here's a list of descriptive words to further help you understand and discuss the matter:

**Abstract**: meaning theoretical or vague
**Absurd**: illogical; ridiculous; silly; implausible; foolish
**Accusatory**: suggesting someone has done something wrong; complaining
**Acerbic**: sharp; forthright; biting; hurtful; abrasive; severe
**Admiring**: approving; think highly of; respectful; praising
**Aggressive**: hostile; determined; forceful; argumentative
**Aggrieved**: indignant; annoyed; offended; disgruntled
**Ambiguous**: having multiple potential meanings
**Ambivalent**: having mixed feelings; uncertain; in a dilemma; undecided
**Amused**: entertained; diverted; pleased
**Analytical**: inclined to examine things by studying their contents or parts
**Anecdotal**: involving short narratives of interesting events
**Angry**: resentful; enraged
**Animated**: full of life or excitement; lively; spirited; impassioned; vibrant
**Apathetic**: showing little interest; lacking concern; indifferent; unemotional
**Apologetic**: full of regret; repentant; remorseful; acknowledging failure
**Appreciative**: grateful; thankful; showing pleasure
**Ardent**: enthusiastic; passionate
**Arrogant**: pompous; disdainful; overbearing; condescending; vain; scoffing

**Assertive:** self-confident; strong willed; authoritative; insistent

**Articulate:** able to express your thoughts, arguments, and ideas clearly and effectively; writing or speech is clear and easy to understand

**Austere:** stern; strict; frugal; unornamented

**Awestruck:** amazed; filled with wonder/awe; reverential

**Belligerent:** hostile; aggressive; combatant

**Benevolent:** sympathetic; tolerant; generous; caring; well meaning

**Bitter:** angry; acrimonious; antagonistic; spiteful; nasty

**Bland:** undisturbing; unemotional; uninteresting

**Boring:** dull; tedious; tiresome

**Callous:** cruel disregard; unfeeling; uncaring; indifferent; ruthless

**Candid:** truthful; straightforward; honest; unreserved

**Caustic:** biting; corrosive; abrasive; critical

**Cautionary:** gives warning; raises awareness; reminding

**Celebratory:** praising; pay tribute to; glorify; honor

**Chatty:** informal; lively; conversational; familiar

**Cinematic:** having the qualities of a motion picture

**Circuitous:** taking a long time to say what you really mean when you are talking or writing about something; not being forthright or direct

**Classical:** formal; enduring; standard; adhering to certain traditional methods

**Clean:** unoffensive language, especially because it does not involve sex

**Colloquial:** characteristic or ordinary and informal conversation

**Comic:** humorous; witty; entertaining; diverting

**Compassionate:** sympathetic; empathetic; warm-hearted; tolerant; kind

**Complex**: having many varying characteristics; complicated
**Compliant**: agree or obey rules; acquiescent; flexible; submissive
**Concerned**: worried; anxious; apprehensive
**Conciliatory**: intended to placate or pacify; appeasing
**Concise**: using very few words to express a great deal
**Condescending**: having a superior attitude; patronizing
**Confessional**: characterized by personal admissions of faults; used more recently to describe very personal, autobiographical writing
**Confused**: unable to think clearly; bewildered; vague
**Contemptuous**: expressing contempt or disdain
**Conventional**: ordinary; usual; conforming to established standards
**Conversational**: informal, like a private conversation
**Cool**: unaffected by emotions, especially anger or fear
**Crisp**: clear and effective
**Critical**: finding fault; disapproving; scathing; criticizing
**Cruel**: causing pain and suffering; unkind; spiteful; severe
**Curious**: wanting to find out more; inquisitive; questioning
**Cynical**: a tendency to believe that all human behavior is selfish and opportunistic
**Decadent**: marked by a decay in morals, values, and artistic standards
**Declamatory**: expressing feelings or opinions with great force
**Defensive**: defending a position; shielding; guarding; watchful
**Defiant**: obstinate; argumentative; contentious
**Demeaning**: disrespectful; undignified
**Depressing**: sad; melancholic; discouraging; pessimistic
**Derivative**: coming from something or someone else (as in the style of another writer)

**Detached**: aloof; objective; unfeeling; distant
**Diffuse**: wordy; difficult to understand
**Dignified**: serious; respectful; formal; proper
**Diplomatic**: tactful; subtle; sensitive; thoughtful
**Disapproving**: displeased; critical; condemnatory
**Discursive**: including information that is not relevant to the main subject
**Disheartening**: discouraging; demoralizing; undermining; depressing
**Disparaging**: dismissive; critical; scornful
**Direct**: straightforward; honest
**Disappointed**: discouraged; unhappy because something has gone wrong
**Dispassionate**: impartial; indifferent; unsentimental; cold; unsympathetic
**Distressing**: heart-breaking; sad; troubling
**Docile**: compliant; submissive; deferential; accommodating
**Dreamlike**: having the characteristics of a dream
**Dreary**: depressing; dismal; boring
**Earnest**: showing deep sincerity or feeling; serious
**Earthy**: realistic; rustic; coarse; unrefined; instinctive; animal-like
**Economical**: efficient with words
**Egotistical**: self-absorbed; selfish; conceited; boastful
**Elegiac**: expressing sorrow or lamentation
**Elliptical**: obscure; suggesting what you mean rather than saying or writing it clearly
**Eloquent**: expressing what you mean using clear and effective language
**Empathetic**: understanding; kind; sensitive
**Emphatic**: using emphasis or boldness in speech or writing, or action
**Encouraging**: optimistic; supportive

**Enthusiastic:** excited; energetic
**Epigrammatical:** a tendency to make use of epigrams, which are terse, witty, or pointed sayings
**Epistolary:** relating to the writing of letters
**Euphemistic:** softened, indirect, innocuous expressions are used for talking about unpleasant or embarrassing subjects without mentioning the things themselves
**Evasive:** ambiguous; cryptic; unclear
**Evocative:** having the ability to call forth memories or other responses
**Excited:** emotionally aroused; stirred
**Experimental:** inclined to try out new techniques or ideas
**Facetious:** inappropriate; flippant
**Farcical:** ludicrous; absurd; mocking; humorous and highly improbable
**Fashionable:** comforting to whatever the current fashion is in language, manners, and/or literature
**Fatalistic:** believing that everything that happens is destined, and therefore, out of the hands of the individual
**Flamboyant:** conspicuously colorful or bold
**Flippant:** superficial; glib; shallow; thoughtless; frivolous
**Flowery:** the use of complicated words that are intended to make it more attractive
**Fluent:** expressing yourself in a clear and confident way, without great effort
**Forceful:** powerful; energetic; confident; assertive
**Formal:** respectful; stilted; factual; following accepted styles/rules
**Frank:** honest; direct; plain; matter-of-fact
**Frustrated:** annoyed; discouraged
**Gentle:** kind; considerate; mild; soft
**Ghoulish:** delighting in the revolting or the loathsome

**Gimmicky:** tricky, sometimes excessively, as in contrived endings

**Grandiloquent:** pompous; haughty; expressed in extremely formal language to impress people, and often sounding overbearing or silly because of this

**Grim:** serious; gloomy; depressing; lacking humor; macabre

**Gullible:** naïve; innocent; ignorant

**Hard:** unfeeling; hard-hearted; unyielding

**Heavy:** profound or serious

**Heroic:** bold; altruistic; like a hero

**Humble:** deferential; modest

**Humorous:** amusing; entertaining; playful

**Hypercritical:** unreasonably critical; hair splitting; nitpicking

**Hysterical:** uncontrollably or violently emotional, whether with fear or rage or laughter

**Idiomatic:** expressing things in a way that sounds natural

**Impartial:** unbiased; neutral; objective

**Impassioned:** filled with emotion; ardent

**Imploring:** pleading; begging

**Impressionable:** trusting; child-like

**Inane:** silly; foolish; stupid; nonsensical

**Inarticulate:** not able to express clearly what you want to say; not spoken or pronounced clearly

**Incensed:** enraged; riled; exasperated

**Incoherent:** without logical connections; difficult to understand

**Incredulous:** disbelieving; unconvinced; questioning; suspicious

**Indignant:** annoyed; angry; dissatisfied

**Informal:** usually referring to register; used about language or behavior that is suitable for using with friends but not in formal situations

**Informative:** instructive; factual; educational
**Inspirational:** encouraging; reassuring
**Intense:** earnest; passionate; concentrated; deeply felt
**Intimate:** familiar; informal; confidential; confessional
**Ironic:** characterized by an unexpected turn of events; often the opposite of what was intended
**Irreverent:** showing disrespect for things that are usually respected or revered
**Jaded:** bored; having had too much of the same thing; lacks enthusiasm
**Joyful:** positive; optimistic; cheerful; elated
**Journalistic:** characterized by the kind of language usually used in journalism
**Judgmental:** critical; finding fault; disparaging
**Juvenile:** immature or childish (can be a fault as in with adults, or meaning intended for children)
**Laudatory:** praising; recommending
**Learned:** a learned piece of writing shows vast knowledge about a subject, especially an academic subject
**Light-hearted:** carefree; relaxed; chatty; humorous
**Literary:** involving books or the activity of writing, reading, or studying books; relating to the kind of words that are used only in stories or poems, and not in normal writing or speech; a form of writing with the goal of producing art rather than entertainment for the masses
**Loving:** affectionate; showing intense, deep concern
**Lyrical:** intense; spontaneous; musical
**Macabre:** gruesome; horrifying; frightening
**Malicious:** desiring to harm others or to see others suffer; ill-willed; spiteful
**Mean**-spirited: inconsiderate; unsympathetic
**Melodramatic:** having the characteristics of melodrama, in

which emotions and plot are exaggerated and characterization is shallow

**Metaphorical:** making use of metaphors, which are figures of speech; nonliteral comparisons

**Metaphysical:** preoccupied with abstract things, especially the ultimate nature of existence and reality

**Minimalist:** inclined to use as few words and details as possible

**Mocking:** scornful; ridiculing; making fun of someone

**Monotonous:** tiresome or dull because of lack of variety

**Mournful:** feeling or expressing grief

**Mystical:** having spiritual or occult qualities or believing in such things

**Naïve:** innocent; unsophisticated; immature

**Narcissistic:** self-admiring; selfish; boastful; self-pitying

**Nasty:** unpleasant; unkind; disagreeable; abusive

**Negative:** unhappy; pessimistic

**Nostalgic:** inclined to long for or dwell on things of the past

**Objective:** uninfluenced by personal feeling; seeing things from the outside, not subjectively

**Obscure:** unclear; indistinct; hard to understand

**Obsequious:** overly obedient and/or submissive; fawning; groveling

**Ominous:** indicating or threatening evil or danger, as dark clouds indicate that a storm is coming

**Optimistic:** hopeful; cheerful

**Ornate:** using unusual words and complicated sentences

**Orotund:** containing extremely formal and complicated language intended to impress people

**Outraged:** angered and resentful; furious; extremely angered

**Outspoken:** frank; candid; spoken without reserve

**Parenthetical:** not directly connected with what you are

saying or writing
**Parody:** a satirical imitation of something serious
**Pathetic:** expressing pity, sympathy, tenderness
**Patronizing:** condescending; scornful; pompous
**Pejorative:** expresses criticism or a bad opinion of someone or something
**Pensive:** reflective; introspective; philosophical; contemplative
**Persuasive:** convincing; influential; plausible
**Pessimistic:** seeing the negative side of things
**Philosophical:** interested in the study of the basic truths of existence and reality; inclined to have a calm and accepting attitude toward the realities of life
**Picturesque:** unusual; interesting; striking
**Pithy:** short and effective
**Playful:** full of fun and good spirits; humorous; jesting
**Poetical:** having the qualities of poetry, such as pleasing rhythms or images
**Polemical:** involving a controversial argument or disputation
**Political:** involved in politics; contains characteristics of propaganda
**Pompous:** displaying one's importance in an exaggerated way
**Ponderous:** serious; weighty; laborious; boring
**Portentous:** trying to seem very serious and important to impress people
**Pragmatic:** preferring practical action and consequences to theory and abstractions
**Precious:** being affected in matters of refinement and manners, sometimes ridiculously so
**Pretentious:** having and displaying an exaggerated view of one's own importance

**Profound**: insightful; deep
**Prolix**: verbose; long-winded; rambling
**Psychological**: having to do with human mind and human behavior
**Punchy**: terse; clear; effective; succinct
**Puritanical**: strict or severe in matters of morality
**Rambling**: long, wordy, and confusing
**Readable**: clear and able to be read
**Realistic**: accurate; authentic; inclined to represent things as they really are
**Regretful**: apologetic; remorseful
**Repetitious**: tediously repeating the same thing
**Resentful**: aggrieved; offended; displeased; bitter
**Resigned**: accepting; unhappy
**Restrained**: controlled; quiet; unemotional
**Reverent**: showing deep respect and esteem
**Righteous**: morally right and just; guiltless; pious; god-fearing
**Rhetorical**: communicating through writing with literary devices and compositional techniques; sometimes thought contrived or pretentious
**Rhythmic**: characterized by certain patterns, beats, or accents
**Romantic**: having feelings or thoughts of love; when associated with nineteenth-century literature or any such literature, it suggests a style that emphasizes freedom of form, imagination, and emotion
**Rough**: incomplete
**Roundly**: complete; in a strong and clear way
**Sarcastic**: inclined to use nasty or cutting remarks that can hurt people's feelings
**Sardonic**: mocking; taunting; bitter; scornful; sarcastic
**Satirical**: using sarcasm and irony, often humorously, to

expose human folly
**Scathing:** critical; stinging; unsparing; harsh
**Scornful:** expressing contempt or derision; scathing; dismissive
**Sensationalistic:** provocative; inaccurate; distasteful
**Sensuous:** taking pleasure in things that appeal to the senses
**Sententious:** expressing opinions about right and wrong behavior in a way that is intended to impress people
**Sentimental:** expressing tender feelings, sometimes excessively, hence the phrase "sloppy sentimentality"
**Shakespearean:** using words in the way that is typical of Shakespeare's writing
**Sharp:** precise; biting; harsh
**Sincere:** honest; truthful; earnest
**Skeptical:** disbelieving; unconvinced; doubting
**Solemn:** not funny; in earnest; serious
**Sophisticated:** worldly and experienced; intricate or complex. In writing, a sophisticated style may suggest complexity or considerable experience in the craft.
**Stark:** plain; harsh; simple; bare; bleak; grim
**Stilted:** very formal, sometimes excessively, as in stilted prose
**Stylistic:** relating to ways of creating effects, especially in language and literature
**Subjective:** relying on one's own inner impressions, as opposed to being objective
**Submissive:** compliant; passive; accommodating; obedient
**Subtle:** delicate in meaning, sometimes elusively so
**Succinct:** expressed in a very short but clear way
**Sulking:** bad-tempered; grumpy; resentful; sullen
**Superficial:** shallow; trivial; dealing only with the surface of things

**Surrealistic:** stressing imagery and the subconscious; sometimes distorting ordinary ideas to arrive at artistic truths
**Symbolic:** using material objects to represent abstract or complex ideas or feelings
**Sympathetic:** compassionate; understanding of how someone feels
**Thoughtful:** reflective; serious; absorbed
**Tolerant:** open-minded; charitable; patient; sympathetic; lenient
**Tragic:** disastrous; calamitous
**Trite:** stale; worn out
**Turgid:** complicated and difficult to understand
**Unassuming:** modest; self-effacing; restrained
**Uneasy:** worried; uncomfortable; edgy; nervous
**Unprintable:** used for describing writing or words that you think are offensive
**Urbane:** sophisticated; socially polished
**Urgent:** insistent; saying something must be done soon
**Vague:** unclear; indefinite; imprecise; ambiguous
**Venomous:** poisonous; malicious
**Verbose:** using more words than necessary
**Vindictive:** vengeful; spiteful; bitter; unforgiving
**Virtuous:** lawful; righteous; moral; upstanding
**Well-turned:** expressed well
**Whimsical:** inclined to be playful, humorous, or fanciful
**Witty:** being able to perceive and express ideas and situations in a clever and amusing way
**Wonder:** awestruck; admiring; fascinating
**Wordy:** using more words than necessary to say what you have to say
**World-weary:** bored; cynical; tired
**Worried:** anxious; stressed; fearful
**Wretched:** miserable; despairing; sorrowful; distressed

# SIX
## GENRE CONVENTIONS
*Give 'em What They Want!*

~

Genre in French means *kind, sort, style*. So when speaking of genre in a literary aspect, the word refers to a broad subdivision of literature. This can be prose, poetry, and drama (novels, poems, and plays). Prose is the most common form of writing and is further broken down into categories such as fiction and nonfiction. We will be covering fiction. You can go even further and categorize fiction into subgenres and sub-subgenres. For purposes of this guide, I'll discuss some popular subgenres (and will refer to them here on out as simply category) and the conventions associated with them.

So, what do I mean when speaking of conventions? Conventions are the defining elements of any genre. They are the universal or agreed expectations of story structure, style, and/or subject matter. A super simplistic example would be that a reader will expect to find a cowboy in a western, some sort of monster or super scary element in a horror, a pair of folks with physical attraction in a romance. It's like a set of blueprints that a writer can follow. That blueprint assures they will write what a reader expects; however, the author's creative spin promises that the story won't be predictable.

An important thing to note here is that there is a difference between expected and predictable. The mystery reader expects to be presented with a mystery to solve from the get-go. They expect to enjoy the trail of clues that leads them to a satisfactory ending. Where the difficulty lies (for the author) is providing that expectation but in a way that stands out from all the other writers' novels that follow those conventions. It's like a chili cookoff. You've got the standard ingredients and a pot. One creative cook will hit the jackpot with the perfect mix of spices and stand out from the crowd. But should he veer too far out in left field, say throw in cream and some cheese and then bake it...well, he's gone too far. He's now in casserole territory. The same can happen in fiction. You can have the elements of a romance with two passionate love birds, but if in the end one kills the other in the heat of passion after learning a shocking secret, well then, you've left romance territory. It may be an interesting twist, but it doesn't adhere to the romance genre conventions.

> **An important note on this: An author can write a novel however she chooses—that is the beauty of the creative liberty afforded with self-publishing—but she must know that exiting the standard conventions will mean potential changes in her genre/category labeling and marketing approach.**

Why are conventions important to know? Because readers are sometimes seeking a particular experience, and a loyal genre reader will most definitely expect that particular experience, whether it be the satisfying happily-ever-after ending in a romance or the comfort in knowing their YA novel is free of explicit and raunchy "love" scenes. An example of incorrectly labeling a genre or drifting from conventions can be easily understood in film. Say you decided you want to go see a chick flick with a group of your girlfriends. Halfway through the movie, a gruesome and graphic murder scene occurs. You are jolted, shocked, maybe a little pissed, right? This is not what you signed up for. Watching a bloody and brutal murder is not how you planned to spend your night with the Keno gals! The same is true for books.

Genre not only involves an author following a set of conventions to adequately categorize the work, but it also plays a huge role in reader response. Readers are conditioned to respond a certain way to certain genres. Reading a fantasy novel? You won't require too much suspension of disbelief. Reading a horror where tons of people get mutilated? Seems natural, right? This is because we are conditioned to have these expectations and responses. Knowing these conventions, as a writer, will serve to help maintain focus and efficiency as well as market the novel appropriately. For the beta reader, knowing these conventions can help you form your analysis and feedback to assist the author in achieving their writing, publishing, and marketing goals.

The standard convention that all the main categories share is a plot-driven story. Aside from that, each has their own conventions to single them out from the pack.

Remember, these conventions are here to serve as a guide, but since mainstream fiction somewhat transcends popular novel categories, the author has the creative liberty to break some rules. As a beta reader, you need to know what conventions are expected by readers before you can identify how and if they are being broken, and whether the author is pulling it off successfully. And while creative liberty has its place in mainstream fiction, it is important to note that it is not experimental in the grander sense. This would push the novel more toward a literary fiction style (basically doesn't fit nicely into any genre) and would therefore need to be classified and marketed as such. So let's cover some of the most popular categories you'll be encountering as a beta reader.

## ROMANCE

*Light-headed. Butterflies. Falling desperately, hopelessly in love.*

If your reading heart beats for a good Romance novel, you're in good company. Romance is the number one category of fiction sold on Amazon Kindle. That means it's a goldmine of opportunity for writers. There are over 400,000 Romance titles listed as of this writing. The Romance fiction industry is worth $1.08 billion dollars according to the Romance Writers of America®. Romance tops the Amazon Kindle highest selling bestseller list and generates regular readers at more than 29 million in the U.S. alone. This is one heck of a loyal audience. And because of this, I would say that Romance is most definitely the category with the strictest of convention expectations from its readers. If the author intends to veer from the standard conventions, I would be sure to let them know to clearly establish this for their readers with appropriate category selection/tags when publishing to avoid scathing reviews from disappointed readers. But if they are aware of the variances in their story, there are no less than—wait for it—sixty subcategories of Romance that they can further label their work. Having said that, here are the expected conventions of the traditional Romance novel:

- an interesting plot with a love story at its heart (two lovebirds meet, one loses the other, gets them back in the end—every. single. time.)
- a sympathetic heroine
- a strong hero that the reader can't resist

- a believable conflict with emotional tension
- a happy ending

See, it's straightforward. And veering from these is not recommended. Statistics show that the Romance genre is the number one selling genre of fiction. Its audience is predominately women—84 percent in fact. And those women are primarily Southern middle-aged, middle-class gals. Statistics also show that these women average buying Romance novels at least once a month and have been doing so for at least twenty years. If you do the math, that's about 240 books that any given reader has read. I think it's safe to say she knows the genre and has expectations.

Now, just to be able to check off these items is not enough. The reader would like a great novel, not just a formula on pages. So here are a few other considerations to keep in mind:

**Word count:** Traditional Romance is 70,000 to 100,000 words; subgenres can run 40,000 to 100,000 words.

**Point of view:** typically written in third person

**Setting:** Knowing that the ending is expected, why not give the reader some variety with the setting? A setting can help the novel stand out.

**Time:** typically past tense

**Plot:** friends become lovers; you are my soulmate—it's fate; second-chance love; secret romance; first love (There are more, but these are the most common.) A writer has the creative freedom to explore as may subplots as he/she wants, but the central love story must remain the focus.

**Pace:** The storyline needs good momentum. The reader needs the action to keep them turning the pages. A solid struggle to make the relationship work (conflict) is key to this momentum.

**Characters:** The heroine should be someone the average reader will love to spend time with; that is, someone that she can relate to. Her hero should be irresistible but not perfect. He needs a growth arc and depth. Make sure these characters' motivations are apparent and serve to further develop their stories.

**Sex:** Sex is often (but not necessarily) a big part of a Romance novel. If it is included, the author must remember who the audience is, and that audience typically wants emotion, not just meaningless sex. And even if it is not included, the author must convey physical attraction between the two, or the reader will bail.

**Emotional payoff:** This is a must. These readers are looking to feel. After journeying with the couple who has struggled for pages upon pages against all odds, the Romance reader wants to be rewarded with emotional justice, the warm fuzzies, the feel-goods.

Because the Romance reader knows what to expect regarding the outcome—happily ever after—the work must provide the conflict and tension in other areas. When reviewing the work, the beta reader should be able to identify the answers to these very important questions:

- What do the characters want and how do their goals bring them into conflict? They each have internal (feelings) goals and external (actions) goals, but these goals conflict with that of the other character. What are they?
- What will they lose if they don't reach their goals? To be considered a loss, it must be meaningful to the person.
- Are their actions realistic when working toward these goals? The author must not "turn off" the

romance reader with outlandish and unbelievable actions.

If these formulaic expectations seem somewhat restrictive and limiting to the creative process, the Romance subgenre/category option is the antidote. The author has the creative authority to grant the novel any style, tone, setting, time period, and subplots her heart desires. Here are a few distinctions to give the standard conventions a creative edge:

**Contemporary Romance:** set from 1950 to the present with a primary focus on the relationship

**Historical Romance:** set prior to 1950

**Suspense Romance:** suspense, thriller, and mystery elements are an integral piece of the plot

**Erotic Romance:** includes explicit sexual interaction that is necessary for the relationship arc

**Spiritual Romance:** includes religious or spiritual elements that are necessary for the relationship arc

**Paranormal Romance:** plot includes fantasy, paranormal, and/or science fiction elements

**Young Adult Romance:** young adult life is an integral part of the plot


The makings of a successful Romance can be found when the author sticks to the standard conventions, spices those conventions up with subcategory creativity, and then markets accordingly within those categories.

**Subcategories of Romance:**
Contemporary • Clean & Wholesome • Fantasy • Sci-Fi • Gothic • Historical Romance • Inspirational • LGBT • Multicultural & Interracial • New Adult & College • African-American • Collections and Anthologies • Paranormal • Romantic Comedy • Time Travel • Western • Military • Holidays • Sports • Mystery • Suspense

These are the main twenty subcategories of Romance. As I said before, there are TONS of Romance authors and titles out there. Opportunities abound, my friend. So if your reading preference is Romance, you've hit the jackpot!

**MYSTERY/THRILLER/SUSPENSE**

*Exhilaration. Fear. Apprehension. The rush.*

Mystery/Thriller/Suspense is the second highest selling category (actually broken down into four main categories consisting of Mystery, Thriller, Suspense, and Crime) in Amazon Kindle with over 250,000 titles listed in thirty-nine subcategories at the time of this writing. Regarding reader expectations of genre structure and convention, I would say that the general M/T/S genre falls next in line behind romance. And while there are some lofty expectations from readers as far as conventions go, the author has the challenge of creating the subtleties that differentiate one category from the next. (An example would be that you wouldn't expect to find a Cozy Mystery within the Phycological Thriller category.) So let's see how we can kind of deconstruct these subtleties.

## MYSTERY

So what's the general understanding of the Mystery novel? A crime is committed—almost always a murder—the journey to discover the details of the crime make up the action of the story: who did it? why? and then the pursuit of justice. The overall (very generalized) theme is discovering the truth. The Mystery reader is looking for an intellectual challenge. Their goal is to solve a mystery before the sleuth, and they dive into a novel with the expectation that everything will come together in the end. This is very important to the reader, and the author should take the responsibility of meeting these expectations seriously to avoid losing a reader and gaining poor reviews.

> **Note: I bet you're thinking romance has a stronghold on the gal readers and writers out there, huh? Not so. If you consider that the oh-so-awesome female readers of the world have come to dominate fiction, representing an impressive 75 percent of the most active e-readers, and that the Mystery/Thriller/Suspense category is pushing at the top ranks of the bestseller lists on Amazon Kindle, well, I'd say move over guys. The ladies are taking this riveting genre by storm! I mean, there's even guys out there who are pretending to be women to get better sales. Not lying, y'all!**

Even though the statistics show that Mystery/Thriller/Suspense is no longer dominated by men, the conventions have remained tried and true.

Plot rules above all else and is centered around solving a mystery—dramatic opening introduces a mystery to hook the reader, protagonist takes on the challenge to solve the mystery, and a resolution occurs with a climactic logical conclusion. Here are the basic plot elements:

- The crime has already happened or happens early in the novel and is dramatic (something the reader will care enough about to devote some 300 pages to).
- The sleuth (investigator of some kind) must be met with conflicts, roadblocks, setbacks, while on the quest to solve the mystery. This character should face both internal and external conflicts.
- The villain is hidden (typically with some type of cover-up).
- The protagonist's (sleuth's) investigation includes the discovery and elimination of suspects.
- By the end, the main character has completed the quest, solved the mystery, and faced the underlying internal conflict.

That's mystery in a nutshell.

As with the other genres, readers have expectations of the Mystery story. Here are a few other considerations to keep in mind:

**Protagonist or hero:** This can be anyone from a journalist, a professional detective, or even a curious busybody. The key is that this person must possess a significant desire to see justice served. This person is naturally gifted with not only a great mind but also great empathy—captivated not with the criminal act, per se, but with the human behind such an act.

**Antagonist or villain:** The crime may have been by chance or an intricately staged act; deceit is the name of the game and comes in the form of a cover-up. Thwarting and escaping justice is the villain's core-defining characteristic. The Mystery villain is smart, a mind-magician, and thrives on blurring the lines between fact and fiction.

**Setting**: Obviously a Mystery can occur any old place, but the setting needs to thematically contribute to the whole of the work. The setting can be used to infuse tone into a work. Oftentimes, what works well is when the setting becomes layered—the crime peeling back and revealing the true nature of the story. So a work can start off in a seemingly normal small town, but as the sleuth gets deeper and deeper into the mystery, the peeled layers of the setting create anticipation and hidden messages. The description of settings, how the words change when describing one setting from the next, also contributes to the tone. Small towns are often used in Mysteries, as they appear on the surface to represent a simple way of life. As the mystery unfolds, secrets and crime shatter the innocent façade.

**Reveals**: The Mystery is all about the big reveal. With the ultimate goal of discovering the truth, the best part of a Mystery is that big reveal. But just as the saying goes, it's the journey, not the destination—sometimes the twists and turns and false leads make the destination that much sweeter!

**Word count**: Mysteries are typically about 75,000 to 100,000 words with the Cozy being slightly less.

The key difference between a Mystery and a Suspense or Thriller is mainly in the delivery. In a Mystery the protagonist doesn't know who the killer is until the end, and the reader gets to join in on solving the puzzle. It's a bit more cerebral for the reader as they take in the clues just a step behind the sleuth.

## SUSPENSE

In a Suspense, the reader may or may not know whodunnit right up front, and she may get to enjoy being one step ahead of the sleuth; that is, she knows things the protagonist may not yet know—perspective is a big distinction between the Mystery and the Suspense. The main emphasis is the anticipation of what could happen. The book progresses at a slightly slower pace and usually enthralls the reader with an overall sense of danger and suspense as they anticipate the protagonist taking in the clues and coming dangerously close to harm's way. The Suspense sometimes employs the villain's point of view.

Additional things to consider:

**Protagonist or hero**: Because the story is usually building up to a crisis and the reader is given a somewhat omniscient perspective, the protagonist needs to be a strong one who can hold her own and keep forward momentum in the face of the unknown. She also needs to have setbacks or some sort of loss to keep the suspense high for the reader.

**Antagonist or villain**: One simple solution for adding suspense to a novel is by making the protagonist's obstacles dangerous; this can be taken care of by the evil villain.

**Setting**: Scenery, the weather, the time of day—all these things can create an atmosphere of suspense. *It was a dark and stormy night.* Need I say more? I kid. Just keep in mind that setting is always important in a Suspense and, if used properly, it can keep the reader right at the edge of her seat. The setting itself can serve as a danger to the protagonist or simply serve as a backdrop to the story.

**Word count**: expected to be in the 70,000 to 90,000 range

## THRILLER

Regarding the Thriller, you may or may not get to see the crime unfold, but you're thrilled by the intense chase of seeing if the villain can be stopped. Oftentimes the protagonist is charged with stopping some type of devastating event. The journey is more like a race against time before the bomb explodes or before the killer strikes again. The reader gets drawn into the cat-and-mouse game between the hero and the villain. There are riveting action scenes that rush forward at break-neck speeds toward that moment of an adrenaline-flooded climax. Thrillers also tend to focus on a particular profession such as law, medicine, or espionage.

Other considerations to keep in mind:

**Protagonist or hero**: The tension is created by the villain(s) placing the hero (and possibly other characters) in danger. The protagonist is oftentimes an underdog in a sense, someone who is psychologically vulnerable, has a lot to lose, has a lot of baggage, but also has the skill set to handle the blows that come from the villain. This can be the newly divorced cop, a lonely trained assassin, or an ex-military man who recently had some sort of personal crisis. To keep the story interesting, the protagonist's known wants and fears are revealed early on. This gives the villain something to work with.

**Antagonist or villain**: In Thrillers, the villain is often the driving force of the story, the catalyst. This can be one person or a group. The villain relentlessly zeros in on the hero and attacks those vulnerabilities that were revealed to the reader early on.

**Setting**: The setting for a Thriller will rely heavily on the type of story and characters involved. Obviously, a Legal Thriller will involve courtrooms and the like. Other settings just need to be written in such a way that they serve the story in a meaningful way. Many times it can be the setting that's at stake if the hero fails, such as in terrorist attacks.

**Word count:** Thrillers can run 90,000 to 100,000 words. They tend to be a bit longer as the writer needs to create for the reader a world that they are unlikely familiar with. Most of us don't know the ins and outs of the medical examiner's world or what a day in the life of a submarine captain might look like. These things take time. But because of this extended time, it is critical that the pace stay fast and thrilling.

**CRIME**

The Crime genre focuses on a sudden imbalance of good and evil and uses a hero and villain to provide an inside perspective for the reader as she follows along and observes the battle. Each side represents the contrasting morals of a given society—one that is just versus one that is corrupt. In the end, order is restored, justice is served, and safety is returned.

Unlike the Mystery novel, there is really no need to discover the bad guy. The story begins with a crime performed by the brilliant villain and then continues like a game of intense chess, the tension building with each move. The key is in the suspense of which side will prevail.

Additional considerations:

**Protagonist or hero:** typically, someone who feels strongly drawn to uphold moral code, to right all the wrongs. This is often an officer of the law or even a vigilante. This person has faith in the flawed society in which she lives. Many times, the hero is seen as the black sheep in society.

**Antagonist or villain:** usually an evil genius or brilliant criminal who loathes the same flawed society he shares with the protagonist. Not only is he a threat to the protagonist, he is a threat to all of society.

**Setting:** The setting in Crime novels can be used to serve the overall theme of the story. Typically, these stories occur in urban locales where big city corruption come easily, but any setting can be used as long as it serves to contribute to grounding the theme.

The Mystery/Thriller/Suspense categories overlap and create somewhat hybrid categories such as Mystery-Suspense and Mystery-Thriller. Basically for the Mystery-Suspense, you have a mystery with the detective trying to solve the whodunnit question, but the suspense is added when the reader is further compelled to wait for the big *why*.

With a Mystery-Thriller, you have your mystery or detective story, but the stakes are higher creating a faster and more intense pace. Maybe if the hero doesn't solve the mystery in time, worse things may happen.

The Mystery/Thriller/Suspense category has an extensive breakdown of subcategories. Here are the thirty-nine listed in the Amazon Kindle store:

- **MYSTERY:** African-American • Collections & Anthologies • Cozy • Hard-Boiled • Historical • International Mystery & Crime • LGBT • Police Procedurals • Private Investigators • Series • Traditional Detectives • Women Sleuths
- **THRILLERS:** Assassinations • Conspiracy • Crime • Espionage • Financial • Historical •

Legal • Medical • Military • Political • Psychological • Pulp • Technothrillers • Terrorism
- **SUSPENSE:** Ghosts • Horror • Occult • Paranormal • Political • Psychological
- **CRIME:** Heist • Kidnapping • Murder • Noir • Organized Crime • Serial Killers • Vigilante Justice

**HORROR**

*Dread. Suspense. Fear. Evil. Irrational.*

Horror—I call it the paradoxical genre. Fear is one of the strongest and oldest emotions known to mankind. And in the real world, we avoid fear like the plague. But in literature, the numbers say that readers flock to these repulsive, violent, and dreadful stories—we flock to the plague. We willfully opt to take a walk on the dark side.

In Horror, fear is the name of the game. The terrors of the imagination that run wild when presented with the unknown intensify this fear. Horror fiction taps into the anxieties associated with the looming unknown. It is human nature to personify fear: an evil spirit, a monster under the bed, a god, ghost, or villain with insurmountable power.

One thing that the Horror demands of its audience is engagement in a conspiracy that requires the suspension of the everyday rules of life. A strong psychological acceptance of the literary world created by the author is a must, and to achieve this, that author should provide some expected conventions. Most of these adhere to the standard elements of the novel—the opening hook, character building with introduction of a problem, arising complications, intensifying conflicts, crises that culminate into a climactic event followed by a resolution and reflection of the protagonist—but with slight alterations.

The genre of Horror oftentimes has similar qualities as the fantasy or thriller genre and can easily overlap, but they are not one and the same. The key defining element of the Horror is that it homes in on fear, which is a wide and vast topic, but then creates an atmosphere dependent upon that fear. The genre is more geared toward the delivery of the story—one that elicits an emotion of fear with its use of vivid imagery and language—rather than a distinct set of conventions that differs from other genres. A child may fear the unknown in the darkness of their closet. Horror takes that fear, swirls it and twists it and creates a world and characters that summon the darkest corners of that child's imagination. The same is true for adults but on a more sophisticated level. An adult may fear losing a loved one. The Horror takes that fear and creates a world where loss is amplified maybe with some type of super virus or plague.

Additional considerations:

**Protagonist or hero**: typically someone relatable—someone like you and me—who is active and engages in ordinary day-to-day life in the ordinary world. In the midst of this activity, a problem arises and some type of warning is given. Think about all the shows you've watched where you know she shouldn't go investigate that noise in the basement, especially when someone's called her and warned her to flee the house. Silly girl.

**Pace**: Readers want to be kept on the edge of their seats, so the suspense must be kept high and the momentum maintained with action.

**Ending**: Readers find an unexpected and shocking ending to be satisfying.

**Setting**: The setting in Horror novels can be used as an

anchor to the story. It is believable, pulling the reader into the shoes of the protagonist, and serves as the breeding ground between good and evil. It seems that a realistic background provides excellent contrast and intensifies the shock value of the story.

Horror tends to get a bad rap, not unlike romance, and can be met with snobbish opinions, but readership proves that it's more popular than ever. At the time of this writing, the Amazon Kindle platform had over 96,000 titles listed in the Horror category.

**Subcategories of Horror:**
Dark Fantasy • Ghosts • Occult • British & Irish • United States • Vampires • Anthologies

**SCIENCE FICTION/FANTASY**

*Possibility—one word to sum up the SF & F category.*

Imagined futures, alternate pasts, advanced and altered technology, magical worlds, creative characters—these are the makings of Sci-Fi and Fantasy books. Science Fiction and Fantasy (also known as Speculative Fiction) stories have been around seemingly since the dawn of time. And the popularity of getting lost in these highly imaginative worlds only grows with each year. The SF & F genre is the third highest selling category in the Kindle store with over 282,000 titles available as of this writing.

Science Fiction and Fantasy is an umbrella category (like Mystery/Thriller/Suspense) and breaks down into Science Fiction/Fantasy-Science Fiction and Science Fiction/Fantasy-Fantasy with forty-four subcategories between the two of them. And while the two main categories tend to blur and share many of the same characteristics, they are not one and the same. To differentiate, just remember, Sci-Fi is about science, things that are possible in a theoretical sense, though most likely improbable. If there's no overarching element of science in the work, it's not Science Fiction. Fantasy is impossible, plain and simple (though not *every* aspect is impossible). Let's dive a little deeper into each.

**SCIENCE FICTION**

Some say that the best Science Fiction is predictive of our future. There are definitely times where this has seemed the case. Consider how Ray Bradbury's "seashell radios" in *Fahrenheit 451* allowed a person to distance herself from the reality of the day-to-day goings on; or how the people of that world relied on giant telescreens to (falsely) connect to others. Seems so similar to the earbuds and screens and social media we rely on today, right? But Science Fiction doesn't have to always be about the future. I think that good Science Fiction presents the reader with possibilities: possibilities of what effects, real or imagined, science could have on an individual or a society. And sometimes people underestimate Science Fiction thinking it's only about time travel or weird science or warped technology or parallel universes. Yes, these are common elements, but it's so much more than that. It's about how these innovations or concepts have a moral, social, political, cultural, religious, or economic impact on those involved. It engages the reader to contemplate how we humans encounter and react to change. One may think that Science Fiction is all about seeking answers, but in its truest form, it's all about posing questions.

As with any fiction, the writer must adhere to the standard elements of the novel as was discussed at the beginning of this chapter. In addition to the basics, here's a few elements that need to be considered for the Sci-Fi genre:

**Theme:** Most Science Fiction has strong themes of the opposition of reality or the challenge of popular beliefs. These are the overall themes, but there can still be subthemes such as the ones we mentioned in the theme portion of Chapter 5. With these overarching themes that challenge reality, readers are asked to suspend disbelief while in the world of the story; however, the basis of the science must be grounded in actual science—it cannot be entirely unbelievable, or readers will revolt. That is not to say that *every* aspect is in line with these laws and principles, but there must be something the reader can use to work out the specifics.

**Credibility:** Oftentimes, the premise is a concept that has been considered by the scientific community but has not been deemed feasible...yet. These are subjects such as mind control, teleportation, time and universe travel, superpowers, bodily transformation, immortality, and of course aliens. The main key to the science is to be sure the facts are straight; and if some part of the science takes its cue from imagination, be sure it can somehow be relatable or verifiable to facts on Earth. What I mean is to give something totally foreign a familiar element. Here's an example: A lab is experimenting with gene therapy and retroviruses to phase out the cystic fibrosis gene. Cystic fibrosis is a real genetic disorder where a protein known as CFTR that controls the normal movement of sodium (Na), chloride (Cl), as well as water in and out of the cells in various parts of the body is either too abundant or too scarce in the body. This basically means the body is forced to contend with too much mucus. It's a life-threating disease that is most known to cause feelings of drowning from within. This would be a familiar element. We may not be familiar with gene therapy or the facts of cystic fibrosis, but one can easily verify that cystic fibrosis can be treated with gene therapy. In the story, the next generation of babies in the experiment are born. However, after many immediate deaths, scientists soon discover that the babies only breathe in salt water. This is obviously fiction, but since we can tie it to the gene therapy and the physiology of the disease in reality, it allows the mind to suspend disbelief for the story.

**Consistency**: Regarding the suspension of disbelief with fictionalized science, consistency can make or break it. Creating these worlds takes a lot of thought. Creating the science takes a lot of thought and research. Making sure that the two are cohesive and make sense alongside one another is very important to crafting an unforgettable (in a good way) story.

**Setting**: The settings are going to be dependent upon the premise and can take place anywhere from in a future world, outer space, an alternative time period or reality, in a subterranean world or Middle Earth, dystopian or utopian society, an apocalyptic or postapocalyptic world, etc. As with the subject matter, the settings are limitless. They just need to support the plot and theme.

**Characters**: Characters such as aliens, scientists, mutants, warriors, scholars, space pirates, cyborgs, androids, humanoid robots, personified computers, and highly evolved humans also feature prominently in the genre.

**Word count**: 90,000 to 120,000 is typical

Other things to consider:

Because of the nature of Science Fiction, science with a twist, an author can feel inclined to overexplain the world and technology they've built or get too heavy handed with the scientific jargon. Yes, the reader needs to know a thing or two, but outright explanations filled with big fancy words will only turn off a reader. A fine balance is the answer. As a reader, I prefer to be given information in somewhat of a drip format through dialogue and actions as needed throughout the story. An upfront lesson thrown at me will only prompt me to close the book. Feeding this complex information little by little, and only when needed, adds to the suspense of the story, keeps a bit of mystery, and helps to build tension. If all the ins and outs of the fictionalized science and world are offered up as an information dump at the get-go, where would the curiosity be, right?

It is true that the imagination knows no limits when it comes to creating Science Fiction; however, the writer needs to earn the trust of the reader before they can expect them to jump in this complex world with abandon. Because of this, the writer has the challenge of infusing rationality, plausibility, and fact into their imaginative events. This often requires extensive research on the established principles and laws of science and can be challenging for the writer as well as any beta reader or editor working on the project.

**Subcategories of SF & F-Science Fiction:**
Adventure • Alien Invasion • Alternative History • Anthologies & Short Stories • Classics • Colonization • Cyberpunk • Dystopian • First Contact • Galactic Empire • Genetic Engineering • Hard Science Fiction • LGBT • Metaphysical & Visionary • Military • Postapocalyptic • Space Exploration • Space Opera • Steam Punk • Time Travel • TV, Movie, and Videogame Adaptations

## FANTASY

*Make-believe—this is what Fantasy is all about.*

Rooted in myth, founded on legends, Fantasy is as timeless as the moon and stars and seems to appeal to all ages, being one of the few genres in which a single work can be equally and easily enjoyed by both an adult and a pre-teen. A spectacular example of this is the Harry Potter series.

The key (and differentiating) element in Fantasy is the impossibility of the story. Fantasy worlds are created from the imagination of the writer—with elements of the familiar for the reader such as relevant real-world themes. Magic and other supernatural elements are the essence of Fantasy and can be found in the plot, setting, and characters. And one of the greatest benefits of Fantasy being imaginative is that the possibilities are endless, giving an author boundless liberty. From the fairytales of old to the modern fantasies of today, the genre seems to evolve and become redefined with each generation.

Having said that, let's look at a few common conventions found in Fantasy:

**Setting**: World-building is one of the most significant and vital elements of Fantasy fiction and serves as the foundation or core of the story. Probably the most used is the one like Earth's Middle Ages with the culture, architecture, and technology being the same: pre-industrial and medieval. The setting can be completely imagined, an alternative reality, or an actual location.

- An example of a **completely imagined setting** can be found in *The Hobbit*. Here, Tolkien has created the complex world of Middle Earth, inspired by Viking mythology. He takes the reader from the comforts of the Shire, through the tranquil Rivendell in the Valley of the Elves, into the enchanted Mirkwood Forest, to the grim and dangerous Lonely Mountain, and back home to the Shire.

- An **alternative reality** is one that is slightly less complex than a fully imagined one. It is an alternate version of the Earth that we know, a real-world location with a twist, a re-imagined event in history. And though it may be less complex, the author has the added challenge of infusing facts with fantasy. An example of an alternative reality setting is found in the *Harry Potter* series. The story takes place in England with some fictional liberties: Godric's Hollow is the fictional village where Harry and his parents lived.
- An example of an **actual location** can be found in *Miss Peregrine's Home for Peculiar Children*. Jacob's story begins in Florida and then advances to England where he embarks on an adventure that takes him back and forth in time. The settings are real; it's the magic infused within them, within the time loops, and in the characters that makes this a Fantasy.

**Characters:** As with other genres, characters are the heart of the story and what draws the reader in and earns their investment. And true to Fantasy's nature of ultimate possibility, the potential for developing characters is boundless. The cast of characters in Fantasy fiction tends to be larger than other genres and sometimes has more than one main character with a few axillaries. Fantasy relies heavily on the archetypes that embody some sort of universal meaning for the reader. But it is the creativity of the writer that gives these character types depth and complexity.

Here are the main character types found in Fantasy fiction: the protagonist(s), antagonist, the mentor, a sidekick, and very often a love interest. These can come in the form of (respectively) the young heroine sent on a quest with her pals, an evil-turned wizard, the wise shape-shifting teacher, the best-friend hobbit, and handsome magician.

The key is to have engaging and relatable characters that will help the readers ground themselves in an otherwise strange and unknown world.

**Time:** Fantasy can take place in any time, imagined or real.

Other things to consider:

**Symbolism:** The unfamiliar and imagined nature of Fantasy can be made relatable with the use of symbolism. And if used well, symbolism can add depth and meaning to a story. Here are some examples in which symbolism can serve a story well:

- Theme: Oftentimes a mirror or maze or portal or time loop can signify a rite of passage.
- Names: The names of characters and locations can serve as symbols.
- Color: Color has always had deep meaning.
- Objects: Throughout time and in various cultures, objects have held deep meanings (an apple symbolizes temptation; a ring symbolizes commitment).

**Word count:** 90,000 to 125,000 is typical.

**Subcategories of SF & F-Fantasy:**
Action & Adventure • Alternative History • Anthologies & Short Stories • Arthurian • Christian Fantasy • Classics • Coming-of-Age • Dark Fantasy • Dragons & Mythical Creatures • Epic • Fairy Tales • Historical • Humorous • LGBT • Metaphysical & Visionary • Military • Myths & Legends • New Adult & College • Paranormal & Urban • Romantic • Superhero • Sword & Sorcery • TV, Movie, Videogame Adaptations

**WESTERN**

*Rugged journeys. Hope of fresh starts. Dreams of freedom. Unspoiled landscapes.*

Mount up, folks. It's time to head to the Wild Wild West. It seems the Western has its own corner in the American imagination, inhabiting a world of its own. One of the most magnificent and fascinating stories of all time is the settling of the American West. I've heard it said that the Western is the mythology of America; so it's no wonder that it serves as an excellent springboard from which to blaze off some great fiction.

At one point, the Western genre was a booming category of mainstream fiction. That time has passed, in a sense. But that's not to say the Western is dead. It's just been whittled down to a niche market. Unlike the other genres we've covered so far, you won't find Westerns in a category of their own (specifically in the Amazon Kindle store) but rather in related categories—Classics, Teen & Young Adult, Horror, Contemporary Fiction, Genre Fiction, and Western Romance—with a range of subcategories. For instance, if you wanted to check out all the 20,000-plus titles in the Kindle store on Amazon for Westerns related to Genre

Fiction, you would search something like this: Literature & Fiction > Genre Fiction > Westerns. From there, you could further find sub-subcategories in Horror, Classics, and Contemporary Fiction. And then of course some added keywords will further narrow it down.

Historically, the Western told a story of the Old American West with spur-wearing cowboys and revolver-wielding gunslingers. Native Americans, outlaws, lawmen, ranchers, and soldiers are often cast. Elements also can include the iconic hanging tree, symbolically colored horses, lassos, and quenching canteens. The beauty of creativity and imagination is that you can put a spin on just about anything. This has resulted in the evolution of the Western novel. In this day and age, you can find Westerns with a variety of elements borrowed from other genres. For now, let's cover some reader expectations for the traditional Western; that is, set in frontier America in the nineteenth century.

**Setting**: The frontier is somewhat of a relative term when considering the possible subcategories for the Western. Originally, Westerns were always set in the Appalachian Mountains. Later they evolved to anything west of the Mississippi River. The general idea is that the story is set in the American West. The key is to remember that the setting is a place where lawlessness abounds. Specific setting elements can include the open range, an isolated homestead, the saloon, a jail, small frontier towns, Native American villages, etc.

**Facts**: Many readers are Western experts, so fact-checking is a must. Contextual flaws can spoil an otherwise good story for the reader. Consistency and accuracy with dialect, the clothes worn, historical events, the primitive lifestyle and technology, and geographical content are vital.

**Characters**: Readers are expecting those classic characters: the cowboy, outlaw, gunslinger, saloon girl, soldier, etc. Using a character type does not mean having flat characters. As with any novel, the characters should be well developed and relatable for the reader. The protagonist needs to be one gutsy son of a gun or one tough-as-nails gal. This person is expected to have goals and big hurdles along the way. They are often a person of high character, one to be revered, and masterfully control their emotions—no reactive, raging, or boo-hooing star gets the lead role in a Western. Yes, the hero experiences all these emotions, but they control them with grace. Typically, this person is self-taught, self-sufficient, full of integrity, and complete with lots of grit.

**Plot**: Believable plots are important in a Western, but action and adventure are what keeps the pages turning. Survival was pretty much the hot topic in the Wild West. And if you think about living each day with that in mind, you may feel a twinge of anxiety. Like with any genre, conflicts arise time and time again building tension throughout the story. With the Western, these conflicts can come from other characters, the setting, the natural elements, wild critters and beasts—you name it.

**Dialogue**: As I mentioned before, consistency and accuracy are important for the Western reader. During the era of the Old American West, not many folks were educated. Some could not write or read. Of course some could, but just keep in mind that education was mostly in the form of survival lessons, not *readin', writin', and arithmetic*. And while this should be reflected in the dialogue, the dialogue should not be fraught with eye dialect to the point that it distracts the reader. There is a fine line, folks.

Other considerations while reading the Western:

A good life-threatening hook is a terrific way to start off

the Western and draw the reader in to an era like none they've ever experienced!

Keep in mind that the Western has evolved over time, just has America. This includes the individual and societal outlooks of women, Native Americans, and the delivery of justice.

**Potential subcategories/topics of the Western:**
Alternative History • Australian • Black Cowboy (buffalo soldier) • Bounty Hunter • Cattle Drive • Celebrity Western • Civil War • Comedy & Parody • Cowpunk (outrageous cross-genre) • Detective Story Western • Doctor & Preacher • Early Settlement • Euro Western • Fantasy Western • Gothic • Gunfighter • Indian Wars • Inspirational Westerns • Land Rush • Lawmen (Texas Rangers) • Mexican Wars (Texan independence) • Mining & Goldrush • Modern Indians • Mormon • Mountain Men & Trappers • Outlaw • Prairie Settlement • Quest • Railroad • Range Wars (sheep men) • Revenge • Romance • Science Fiction • Town-tamer • Wagon Train • Weird Western • Women

**YOUNG ADULT**

*Life is hard, especially for the adolescent.*

There's no manual for young adulthood (Gosh, wouldn't that help us all?), for how to handle entering a world of greater independence—and greater challenges. So it's no wonder that the Young Adult genre is sometimes referred to as the most important. The coming-of-age theme hallmarks the YA novel, leaving a potentially hefty responsibility for the author whom targets those twelve- to eighteen-year-old readers.

And a quick note regarding that age range. It's one that

folks can't seem to settle and agree upon. Research the targeted age for the Young Adult genre and you'll likely find a few different ranges. In fact, you'll also find that there are blurred lines with categories such as Teen and New Adult in connection with YA. I've seen explanations that Teen refers to ages twelve to fourteen, YA refers to fifteen up to college age (which could be the same as Teen if you're a modern-day Doogie Howser), and New Adult refers to the college years (which is an ambiguous description for an age, right? I mean, I was in college, again, in my thirties. Don't let my attempts at humor muddy the waters here). It's a hot topic out in the interwebs.

So, regarding the distinctions between Teen, YA, and NA, just keep in mind that they are each a general range. The key for YA is that the subject matter must be *interesting* for anyone twelvish and up, not necessarily that they *are* twelve and up. The term "Young Adult" is really about marketing, not so much about a physiological definition of age. The original audience, being adolescents, don't want to read "Adolescent Fiction." They're looking for greater autonomy, right? They want to read about what the older kids are doing. So why not name it YA and call it a day? And that's pretty much the gist.

Common sense plays a role, of course. It's far more appropriate to pitch the book with a campus rape at a drunken frat party to the New Adult audience than to a bunch of twelve-year-olds. Common sense—no special knowledge needed (yet not always easy to come by).

What you can be certain of is that regardless the exact age a book is targeting, it's being read by adults as well. I've run across statistics as high as 55 percent, referring to the percentage of YA novels purchased by adults. The genre is a booming one, regardless who's buying. In fact, it's the fourth highest selling genre in the Kindle store. From 2016 to 2017 there was a 29 percent growth in YA sales with there being approximately 239,000 titles available at the time of this writing. So yeah, people are reading YA. Let's look at what those people are expecting out of this beloved genre.

**Theme:** The possibilities are limitless, but generally YA themes are complex. Most often, they are moral themes. Where trouble can creep in is if a novel becomes "motherly" or "preachy," delivering life lessons *at* the reader. The goal is to unearth questions, not shovel in answers.

**Characters:** Adverse teen protagonists who suffer from teen*ish* problems, which is pretty much every dang thang— puberty, bullying, sex, parents, first love, first breakup, school, friends, alcohol, pregnancy scares (Man, I have zero desire to return to those years)—are the stars of the YA novel. Basically, teen angst is the name of the game for the protagonist. Oh, and they should solve their own problems. No swooping in of an adult of any kind—parent, teacher, neighbor, counselor, etc.—to save the day, or you'll hear groans and books slamming shut from readers across the globe.

**Plot:** Plot and character are king for the YA novel. The plot needs to be a well-oiled machine with continued forward progression. Flowery and fluffy lyrical language may slow down the reading and can be saved for the literary novel. Each sentence must propel the next; therefore, the plot should be strong and with lots of internal and external conflict leading up to a climax that ends with the knowledge that the protagonist (and reader alike) can survive anything with hope on their side.

**POV:** It's common to find first-person point of view in YA novels. Being that the protagonists are most often teens, whom tend to be very self-focused, it makes sense to use first person. The next common POV is third person limited. This is that limited-objectivity point of view where the narrator is close to one of the characters (discussed in Chapter 5), most likely the protagonist. The advantage of using these two POVs is that they create a greater connection between the reader and the character, limiting the narrative distance.

One thing that's tricky with the point of view in the YA novel is getting the right perspective; that is, one that is immediate to the time. Teens can spend time in reflection of their younger years, but they don't have the luxury of adult wisdom via this hindsight. Avoiding "looking back" with an adult perspective can be difficult. Just remember, it should be a story set in the teen years, not looking back on them.

**Language:** It may seem instinctive to talk down to an audience of young teens, but this is a real bust for the YA novel. Dumbing down for this audience is absurd if you think about it. I mean, take one look at a high school AP English reading list and see who feels dumb now. There's no need to alter the writing in this regard.

Cursing is a tough topic too. Teens curse. Well, not all, but many do. And even though the book is meant to engage and relate to adolescents and teens, they are not necessarily the ones choosing—or I should say approving—the books. Parents, teachers, and librarians can act as gatekeepers. Add a few F words here and there, and the book may be shunned by those gatekeepers. Also, slang needs to be highly considered. While it may benefit the Historical YA novel, slang among the teens evolves faster than Madonna. It has a shelf-life. (Case in point: I just dated myself with that Madonna reference.)

Other considerations:

**Word count:** highly flexible; a good starting place for

new authors is 50,000 to 80,000 words. Subcategories such as fantasy and sci-fi can often tack onto the word count due to the world-building nature of these stories.

**Reader proxy:** This is a tool used often in the YA novel, and it helps to gain access to that element of "self" that teens so strongly hold on to. It's when the author writes the protagonist somewhat flatly, allowing the reader to inhabit the character. This is accomplished by not giving too much physical description of the character but rather using generalities as to not alienate a certain type of reader. Giving the protagonist a general and unexceptional description results in leeway for the reader's imagination; the reader can see themselves in this role easier and therefore gains closer proximity to the character. It allows them direct access to the questions that arise for the character.

An example is Bella in *Twilight*. She's completely average. She's got no remarkable skills. She can be anyone—or rather just about anyone can fill her shoes. It makes it easier to get into that strong teenage sense of self the protagonist has.

**Suspense:** I don't necessarily mean a YA novel must be a suspense story, but it does need elements of suspense to keep the audience turning the pages. Well, all stories do, in my opinion. But the YA reader *really* needs that element of anticipation.

**Gravity:** The scenarios in YA novels are rarely unheard of; however, it should be remembered that they are often new experiences for the characters and the younger readers. This, paired with the heightened emotions of adolescence, generates a gravity weightier than the adult novel. This creates an authenticity that readers will appreciate.

**Censorship:** YA gets is fair share of censorship. As with cursing, the terrible and touchy realities that are often part of the YA novel are a target for censorship. This can cause lots of stress for the YA writer. To them, I say simply to write what best serves the reader. I believe if a writer envisions her target audience sitting with her book clutched tightly, the appropriate and authentic words will come. The goal is sincere reflection, not shock value.

**Hope:** The young generation wants hope—needs hope, I should say. (Gosh, and so do we all, right?) So while I'm not saying to avoid the tough subjects, the touchy topics, to have a shiny and clean PG novel, I am saying that YA readers expect a glimmer of hope. This is often found in the ending. After spending time confronting sexuality, relationships, heartache, loss, tragedy, the ugly realities of life, hope of possibility should be the final sendoff.

So there you have it, folks—some of the most popular genres that you'll encounter as a beta reader. I've done my best to point out some key reader expectations for you, since maybe up to this point you hadn't read for any other purpose than sheer entertainment and hadn't noticed. The main thing I want you to remember is that no genre-specific story has to tick off each and every one of these conventions. Remember, it is called creative writing. And there are some out there in the writing world that may frown or disagree with what I've written. And I'm A-Okay with that. Research a bit and you'll find some variances, I'm sure. But what I do know for a fact is that if a writer aims to market a book as a genre and leaves too many of these reader expectations out, they'll (as my daddy would say) find themselves up Shit Creek without a paddle.

Conventions can feel restrictive to a writer, cliché even. But readers want what they want. And if an author doesn't give them what they want, well, then they'll not sell many books.

To these writers concerned about the conventions stifling their inner creative self, I say two things: either market your book as something other than Genre Fiction or embrace the conventions as what they are. After all, they are simply the tried-and-true methods used by writers for years to inform both their storytelling as well as their marketing. If a writer can get on board with that, they'll be able to deliver to readers what they want and expect, and in return those satisfied readers may just tell a friend or two about them.

# PART II RECAP

In this section you have learned

- an interesting fact about Ernest Hemingway
- the basic elements of creative writing (novels)
- what readers expect to get out of a novel when selecting from a specific genre
- the typical conventions found in highly read genres

ROMANCE
MYSTERY/THRILLER/SUSPENSE
HORROR
SCIENCE FICTION/FANTASY
WESTERN
YOUNG ADULT

# PART II RECOMMENDED READING

*The Lie That Tells a Truth: A Guide to Writing Fiction* by John Dufresne

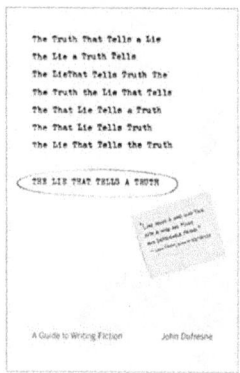

Now, I realize this is supposed to be a guide to writing fiction (and you didn't sign up here to be a writer...but maybe someday?), but what I found is that *The Lie That Tells a Truth* is really *about* writing fiction—about writers, writing, literature, and just the essentials of what makes a good book, not so much an A-Z or formulaic guide. Dufresne's candor and wit and enthusiasm are contagious, and I found it a truly enjoyable read. So if you love to read about how stories get crafted as much as reading the stories themselves, this is a great book. It's like when I read an exceptional book, I'll go all creeper style and learn everything I can about the story, the inspiration for it, the writer, her history, her education, etc. If you're the same, you'll appreciate this recommendation.

# PART III

~

"You fail only if you stop writing."

— RAY BRADBURY

At first glance, you might think this quote would be better suited for a writer who is considering throwing in the towel. But I chose to include this quote for *you* because I want to make it crystal clear that the hardest part of the writing process is not that first or second draft; it's getting the feedback, being able to process it and apply it, and then having the guts to head back to the chopping block. This is hard stuff for a writer. Sending the work out for *you* to read and critique is scary. Getting the feedback and reading that feedback is even scarier. If an author has thin skin, a beta reader's poorly formed opinions, harsh words, or dead-end feedback can shred what little confidence that author has and leave them feeling too vulnerable to proceed. So remember that *your* words and how *you* present them matter...big time. Don't be that person that crushes someone's dream, nudges them closer to quitting. And don't be that person that lets someone walk obliviously into the wolves either (gotta share the difficult truths too). Be a beta reader that serves to support the dreams of the people that create those magical, thrilling, and engaging stories we book junkies love.

"The other six or seven drafts are going to be pure

torture. So why not enjoy the first draft, in the hope that your joy will seek and find others in the world who, reading your story, will catch fire, too?"

— RAY BRADBURY

As a beta reader, let us not ever put out the spark that lives deep in the creative heart of a writer.

∽

### Did you know?

Ray Bradbury is one interesting man. For ten years he wrote at least one short story a week. In his book *Zen In the Art of Writing*, he says that he accomplished this with gusto by writing the first draft of a new story on Monday. He would spend Tuesday through Friday rewriting with a complete new draft on each day. By Saturday, he would mail out the sixth and final draft to the pulp magazines. Sundays were spent in deep thought preparing for the next week's new story.

He wrote *The Fire Man* which later became *Fahrenheit 451* in the basement of the library of the University of California in nine days, spending a dime for each hour needed for a rented typewriter. The total cost for that first draft, one dime at a time, was nine dollars and eighty cents.

So, I wondered how in the world could this seemingly break-neck writing speed possibly equate to anything remotely close to a Zen experience. Thankfully, he addressed that. He expressed that quantity gives experience and that it's experience that renders quality over time...with practice. And that in time this act that is so regarded as work will soon require less stress and effort and agonizing to do; the writer will soon begin to relax; and the words and stories will simply flow.

## SEVEN
## BETA READING ETIQUETTE AND TIPS
*I Always Ask, "What Would Momma Do?"*

~

Beta reading, when done well, can help propel a writer's work in the right direction. If done badly, it can rub someone the wrong way. Here's a few thoughts on the process:

**Don't accept anything you can't give 100 percent of your focus to.** Remember, this is incredibly important for the author—and probably a bit nerve wracking. If you don't truly have the space in your life to give a read your best effort, pass on it. Half-hearted feedback is disappointing at best.

**Identify the author's vision.** The number one result of the entire creative writing, editorial, and publishing process is to have the author's vison realized. To achieve this, each contributing reader, editor, designer, etc., needs to be keenly aware of the author's vision for the work. This means that you must refrain from imposing your personal vision or worldviews onto the writer's story. Use an intake form to get clear on the author's goals from the get-go and stay true to the author's vision with every aspect of your feedback.

**Don't beta read for genres or subjects you don't like;** you'll be wasting everybody's time. Remember, you've opted to pursue beta reading so that you can use your passion in a productive way. Why subject yourself to something you don't like? And more likely than not, you'll struggle to find anything nice to say.

**Be honest.** No one benefits from dishonesty. Use kindness and empathy to express honest feedback, both positive and negative. The writing will benefit, and you'll gain an author that trusts that your opinions are from a place of sincerity and a desire for them to succeed.

**Deliver criticism with the vehicle of praise.** Everyone, even the toughest of folks, needs to know that their efforts have paid off in some way. And even though they've come to you for help identifying areas in their work in need of attention, it's always best received when the author sees that you recognize their strengths and make suggestions for using those strengths to address weaknesses.

**Be specific.** Ambiguous comments help no one. It's like saying drive "that way" to get somewhere and hoping they'll figure out all the turns along the way. Generalities such as "It's good" serve no purpose either. Be specific. Own your comments and questions with reasons why you've presented them.

**Avoid negative absolutes.** While being specific is helpful, negative absolutes give the writer no recourse for the issues you've identified. "The theme is lacking" is concrete, sets the author on the defense, and offers no help. "Your main character is unrelatable" basically just says they've failed at developing a character. Focus your comments and questions on *how* they can use their strengths to provide a "fix."

**Respect deadlines and keep clear communication.** Most writers have deadlines of their own to meet. Oftentimes, they are using multiple beta readers, have put down a deposit for an editing time slot, and of course just want to get this painstaking work done. I always confirm receipt of the work and reiterate the agreed-upon deadline in an email. If the work isn't due for some time, like it's scheduled out a few weeks or so, I'll shoot them an email once I've commenced with the reading. After I've finished and sent the letter and marked-up manuscript, I'll request confirmation that they've received it. You never know what can get lost in virtual space and never want tech issues to cause a delay when you've done your part in meeting the deadline. As with every aspect in life, communication is key.

**Respect the author's guidelines.** Many times beta reading is comprehensive, but you may come across authors who have a specific desire in mind with your service. This is determined with the initial intake form. Remember, this could be their first beta read (early in the process), or this could be after twenty revisions and a round of professional editing. You never know. So be sure you are clear on what the author wants out of this beta read, and as best you can, stick to those guidelines.

**Hang up your personal agenda before taking on a novel.** Never forget that your role is to serve the writer in their desire to achieve the best book possible. That's it. Pet peeves are a personal bias that don't belong in the beta reading process.

**Watch your words.** Keep in mind that your opinions are just opinions. No matter how well-read you are, how much experience you have, you don't hold the key to this person's success. Stay humble during this process with the knowledge that your opinions are not facts. Basically, don't be that know-it-all, condescending jerk that turns everyone off.

**Remember that what you appreciate appreciates.** You are getting to work with stories, writers, books—what better way to give back to this amazing world of books that has given you countless nights of comfort and adventure and inspiration and entertainment and wisdom? Let that gratitude be known to every author that has entrusted you with their work.

# EIGHT
## BETA READER EXPECTATIONS
*Expect a Professional Relationship Above All Else*

Many beta readers read for hobby only. Some, who write, read in exchange for a returned beta read of their own work. Some read for a fee. Whatever the agreement, be clear up front before taking on the work. That way, you'll know what to expect from the author when the project is complete. For hobbyists, authors will often give thanks with cards, a copy of the book, or a gift of some kind. Everyone is different. If anything, sincere appreciation should be expressed to you for the earnest effort and time you've given toward their work. If you aren't shown any form of appreciation, I urge you to hold true to the last etiquette tip I gave: show the writer your gratitude for the opportunity to work with them. Maybe their momma didn't raise them to express appreciation—you could be a shining example. You worry about you. Let their actions reflect their character. I believe that most often, you'll find that authors are truly appreciative of their betas and make it known.

**It's possible that the author will not agree with your feedback.** Some people struggle with accepting any type of criticism, even though they asked for it. You may get further requests to explain yourself. I try to avoid this by being as positive and thorough as possible in my comments and letter, leaving little room for misunderstanding. If you feel you've done the best job you can, been honest, and delivered that honesty in an effective and supportive manner, that's all you can be expected to do. And you can say so. I wouldn't continue any back and forth with anyone who appears closed to criticism or seems intent on defending their writing or attacking your feedback. I'm not saying to just outright ignore them; maybe you didn't clearly express a reason for a comment in your feedback and truly should revisit it. But if it gets to be an excessive amount of continued contact, well then, you've just entered brainstorming or critiquing or coaching territory (or just a battle). You can always kindly say that your opinions are just that and that you are keenly aware that the author is ultimately the one who decides what feedback to accept or ignore. Just say you wish them the best and move on if this is looking like a no-win and no-end situation. I've yet to have anyone be this defensive. I like to think that it's because my feedback, even though sometimes digs deep into the nitty-gritty, still has a tone of optimism for their success.

**You may or may not get any feedback from the author about the service you provided.** We all would like to know if we've helped or not. And you can always ask for any feedback with a brief survey or a few questions in an email. Just know that many writers are juggling the many aspects of getting this work done—and probably alongside another job and their family life—and may not get back to you for some time. Give it a few weeks and then follow up again. Many times saying that you'd appreciate a short testimonial will work. Self-publishing authors are keenly aware of the power of a review or testimonial.

**The author has likely used more than you as a beta reader.** Many use a handful. Don't expect that all your suggestions are going to be acted upon. A lot of writers will want to see that more than one beta felt the same way about something or that an editor has the same suggestion before they make any changes to the story.

**You shouldn't expect to be asked to adhere to unreasonable deadlines** or to consistently correspond about the actual beta read while it's in progress. I avoid all this by being very upfront from the get-go. I agree to a deadline as well as the date which I should expect to receive the project. Once received, I'll confirm receipt, let them know to expect the feedback by the agreed-upon date, and that I'll expect a confirmation of receipt from them once the project and analysis have been sent back. Let them know that you'll not be sending any progress updates during the read, and that if you have any major concerns or issues, you'll contact them. If you do happen to find yourself in a situation where the author keeps contacting you for updates, kindly let them know, again, that it's not your practice to give progress updates as it eats away at your productivity, and that they should expect to hear from you next at the agreed-upon deadline. If they just keep nagging the hell out of you, you can always graciously decline to continue to work with them.

**You are not expected to brainstorm with an author.** You are beta reading. Brainstorming is the job of a critique partner, certain writing coaches, or can be done with a writing group.

**Author autonomy is to be expected.** There is no guarantee that the author will act on your feedback. That is their right. Just know that you've given your best. Resist the urge to push the author to heed your advice. And no matter what, if the author didn't heed your advice, went ahead and published with less-than-stellar results, do not chastise them in any way. We are all human. The author clearly did what they felt was best for them. Respect that and move on.

# NINE
## HELPFUL TEMPLATES AND TOOLS
*For You and Your Clients*

**TEMPLATES**

**Self-Editing Checklist**

*http://www.dedriemarie.com/author-self-editing-checklist*

Download this handy self-editing checklist and save it. Use it to create a new one if you like. A checklist to offer your authors may prove valuable someday, especially when you've come across a manuscript that needs a fair share of revision work. My core purpose for getting into this business is to help authors. If I suggest a self-edit because it's not even beta-ready, then I feel I can best help that author by providing a means to assist with that recommended task of self-editing.

**Nondisclosure Agreement**

*http://www.dedriemarie.com/non-disclosure-agreement*

A nondisclosure agreement (NDA) states that you will not share the author's work with anyone. Self-publishing authors sometime hesitate to give their entire manuscript over for beta reading or editing services. I gladly offer an NDA to put them at ease. Knowing you are not going to steal their story and publish it yourself eases their mind and costs you nothing but a few minutes of your time. Some betas and editors get offended if asked to sign any such thing. It seems silly to get up in arms over one, to me. Just do it, and then you can focus on what really matters: helping the writer get their story as awesome as possible. You're welcome to check out my NDA or download the logo-free sample I've got on my website. I'm no lawyer and cannot advise you in any real way about this matter, so I suggest you check out Rocket Lawyer to gain some insight on legal documents.

**Author Questionnaire for Beta Reading Services**

*http://www.dedriemarie.com/author-questionnaire-for-beta-reading-services*

I always send out an author questionnaire so that I'm mighty clear on the author's goals for the beta read as well as the book overall. Here is one I use. There's a downloadable logo-free version there as well for your use.

**Project Tracking Worksheet**

*http://www.dedriemarie.com/project-tracking-for-the-beta-reader*

I am a stickler about tracking my time and adhering to deadlines. You should be too, unless your goal is to rub a whole bunch of folks the wrong way. It may take some practice to form the important habit of tracking your time (you most likely will have many starts and stops), but it will serve as an effective tool for tracking your work efficiency as well as the flow of the manuscript. I like to provide the author an itemized table of my work which also serves to track time spent on the project. I am a big proponent for justifying any work you've done. Here's my handy-dandy project tracking sheet I use for my beta reads. Hope it helps!

**Character Sketch**

*http://www.dedriemarie.com/character-sketch*

Characters, like real people, have quirks, likes, dislikes, motivations, hang-ups, fears, habits, specific morals, values, and worldviews. A sketch assures that a character evolves while staying true to himself every step of the way. As a reader, if you can't point out how a character evolved throughout the story, you may want to mention this to the author. And of course, you can always send them a character sketch form as an added value and helpful way to address the concern you've raised.

**Professional Readthrough Worksheet**

*http://www.dedriemarie.com/beta-reading-worksheet*

It's helpful to have a worksheet to follow along or review to assure you consider the many aspects of a novel. Sometimes it's easy to focus on a few areas and neglect others. Here's a worksheet with a list of topics to consider that also can serve as a tool to help you organize your thoughts. You don't have to answer every single question, but it's nice to have a vast list of them handy.

**TOOLS**

Regarding tools for beta reading, I recommend one or both of the following: Microsoft Word using Track Changes and/or a tablet with an app to mark up or annotate the work. I subscribe to Office 365 to assure I always have the most up-to-date Word program. And then I have my iPad Mini with Branchfire's iAnnotate app for marking up documents. At the time of this writing, the app was a one-time fee of $9.99. There are apps out there for other tablets, and there are apps out there for free, but I prefer iAnnotate to make and organize my notes, sign agreements (like an NDA), highlight text, insert custom stamps, research information, and more. If you are unsure how to use Track Changes or any type of annotation app for marking up directly on documents, you can always consult Uncle Google or Aunt YouTube for tutorials. Or, if you're anything like me, you just want someone to show you step by step what the heck to do. If so, you'll love the second book in this series, *How to Become a Successful Beta Reader Book 2: Mastering the Art of Crafting Feedback*. It's got a step-by-step chapter for the tech-challenged book junkie.

You may come across some nostalgista who wants to send you a hard copy of their lifelong work. We live in a digital age, but if you find you have the odd desire to play along, I suppose all you will need is a red pencil or pen, some sticky notes, a highlighter, a notebook, and possibly a stiff drink—scratch that, definitely a stiff drink. I don't recommend reading this way, as nostalgic as it sounds, as it can be quite time consuming. I guarantee you will find yourself on a wild and frantic page-flipping hunt if you need to reference something previously mentioned in the manuscript and then can't find it. Picture loose pages... everywhere! Um. Hell. No.

## TEN
## FINAL THOUGHTS
*Getting Your Head in the Game*

Many people struggle to try something new. Many people don't feel they have anything of value to offer. But you are not many people. You are a smart, curious, and voracious reader. You are someone who respects the creativity and diligence that goes into crafting a novel. You are someone who cares about books, about words, about the people behind the book, about the characters within the pages. You are meant to do this. You just hadn't known before that you could. All I've done is unearth the groundwork you've been treading over anyways. So squash that devil sitting on your shoulder saying you can't. Get out there and put your new skill set to use. Help a writer. And be confident in the knowledge that you'll give your best effort to do so. Many newbie betas apologize in advance for their newness and the quality of their critiques, certain they will have no value for the writer. Not true for you. First and foremost, you now have the knowledge to read with a purpose. Have confidence in your opinions. Deliver them with care. That's where a good beta begins.

Many times in my life I've learned a new thing, gotten all jazzed up about that thing, then been suddenly struck with fear about presenting that thing to others. When I first set about interviewing for my first physical therapy job, the thought that I was a complete sham overcame me. Even though I had graduated second in my class, aced my state boards, already had countless patients commend me during my internships, I was overly consumed with doubt. I think the new trendy word for this is imposter syndrome. I was gut-churning anxious, y'all. Fortunately, I had some unconditionally supportive folks in my life that pushed me to act, even though I was scared. And ya know, turned out I'd do well in that career, helping people, growing rehab teams, transitioning into other fields, and building healthcare businesses.

Then when I decided I wanted a change, I pursued work in the literary world. And let me tell you, all that self-doubt crept back up on me. To combat it, I studied my booty off and researched like a banshee (my go-to in life is to acquire knowledge...sometimes the acquisition stalls me actually doing anything; so beware of procrastination disguised as research). I dumped tons of money (that I didn't have) and time (that was equally as scarce) into trying to *feel* confident. And you know what, all that stuff doesn't really work unless you **do something with the knowledge.** Yes, you obviously need to be informed and educated to do good work, but knowledge alone gets you nowhere unless you act.

So that's what I'm pushing you to do. You want to be a beta reader that authors will love and cherish? Well, you have to get out there and get started. Here are my suggestions:

### GET MIGHTY CLEAR ON YOUR GOAL.

Want to build a business working with authors that allows you to work from anywhere in the world (anywhere with electricity and an internet connection...details, details)? Want to gain some super fun skills that you can barter for free books? Want a flexible gig you can tackle part-time while you finish up your degree? Want to become a writer yourself and use beta reading as a way to submerge yourself in the processes of others?

Whatever your goal, be very clear.

#### Figure out your WHY.

My why was because I loved books, loved to travel, loved the idea of autonomy, and a 9-5 job kind of got in the way of all that. So I built an editorial business that allowed me to enjoy reading every day, that I could do when and where I chose.

Yours could be that you too want to become a writer and feel like beta reading would give you some inside perspective. Whatever the reason, get clear on it and revisit your *why* every day. It'll keep you moving forward during the rough patches.

#### Make a plan.

To me, this is the most fun part of any task. I'm a born planner; love it; should probably figure out how to be a professional planner of some sort. I plan out my year in detail. I use Dragontree's Dreambook + Planner (no affiliation, just love the thing).

#### Chunk up those goals into manageable tasks.

And be sure to give them a deadline. Tasks without deadlines can easily pile up on a giant to-do list. I typically write out all the tasks needed to fulfill a goal and then select JUST ONE to complete for a given day. If there's time after that, go for another. But start with just one. It'll help to ease any overwhelming feelings you may have.

For beta reading, maybe your first task can be to join a beta reader or writer group on Facebook to get a feel for that demographic and what the current conversations are. Then your next task could be to introduce yourself.

Or maybe your first task could be to read one short story and do a practice beta read to get some experience without the pressure of delivering. I strongly recommend this, by the way. I 100 percent believe that quantity begets experience which begets quality which begets confidence. A sense of inferiority can oftentimes be the emotional outcome of merely a lack of experience.

### Write those tasks down.

Yes, you have them written in your planner, but now you need to write your one focus task somewhere that stares you in the face: a sticky note on your computer, a screensaver on your phone or computer, tacked up on a corkboard—wherever you can keep this task highly visible.

### Limit your research.

I know I said you need to be informed and educated and to browse the conversations in some groups, but do not allow your time to be consumed with so much research that it basically becomes another form of procrastination. You are new to this beta reading business, I get it. And there are dozens of blogs and such online about the topic (though very few actual comprehensive resources, hence the reason a wrote this three-book series on the topic), but don't get mired in the madness of research to the point of overwhelm.

### Keep an I'ma Gettin' There jar.

Have you ever worked for hours or days or weeks on something and when asked how it's going, you felt like you had little to show? Same here. That's why I've become a HUGE fan of recognizing accomplishments. Make yourself an *I'ma Gettin' There* jar. You can use an old glass hurricane (candle holder) or fish bowl or whatever floats your boat. Slap a label on it. Each day write your focus task on a slip of paper. When completed, wad it up and toss it in. Times where you believe you've not made progress on a big project, look at the rising papers and get some clarity.

You don't have to have a jar, of course. I just like the visual, tangible aspects of accomplishment...and the act of wadding up the paper is like popping bubble wrap for me. I like the sensation; it keeps me motivated.

Keeping a journal or a list to tally can accomplish the same thing. The point is to recognize (and be sure to do this daily) that you are, in fact, making progress.

### Pace your learning and limit it to the appropriate times.

I can't think of any profession or skill that one should learn the final steps before laying some fundamental groundwork first. I certainly didn't learn how to use muscle energy techniques before learning extensively about the musculoskeletal and neurological systems in therapy school. Musicians don't learn composition without first learning how to read music. So don't delay getting started beta reading by trying to become an expert at building an author service business. Learn the fundamentals of what authors write. Learn how to link your opinions to those fundamentals. Then you can tackle learning how to establish your services and feel confident in doing so.

### Believe to receive.

Working with authors is not just for NYC publishing professionals anymore. People like you and I can now enjoy the rewards that come from helping our beloved story crafters pen great novels. Authors are people, just like you and me. They too are working to overcome the fear of putting themselves out there; it's just in a different way. But to do it, they must hold on to the belief that they will succeed. And so should you.

Belief in success requires a kind of faith. And faith is the giving up of all doubt to something unknown, unseen. We all have faith of some sort, right? We do. Hear me out. If you drop a cupcake from a building, you have zero doubt that it will plummet to the ground below. You can't see gravity, but you fully believe it exists. You have faith in the unseen law of gravity. *But this isn't the same, Dedrie. I can at least see the outcome of gravity...see that pink delight splat on the ground.*

It *is* the same. You just haven't given the outcomes of your faith in yourself as much thought, probably since your fifth-grade science teacher didn't test you on it.

Think of a time in your life when you were unstoppable, unwilling to *not* achieve something. Maybe you set your sights on a great guy and ended up marrying him. Maybe you ended a terrible marriage (*that* can take real guts). Maybe you aced an exam at school. Maybe you racked up tons of debt. This all is a result of the faith you have in yourself. I know most people don't believe that they have created the crappy parts of their lives, but they have. What you believe is what you receive. You believe you will fail, you probably will. You believe you will struggle with money all your life and live in debt, you probably are already and will continue to do so. You believe you can't be a beta reader that authors will love, you're right. But if you believe you *can* do something, you'll do it. I'm not saying that means it will magically appear and that it'll be so easy, but your belief will keep you working toward that goal until you've achieved it. So believe in yourself. And why not? What's the alternative? Worst case is you fail a little. Big deal. We all do. Get up, learn from it, and keep going. It's what all the cool cats do.

CELEBRATE THOSE WINS.

And I mean all of them. The best thing you can do for yourself is to champion your journey. Did you request to join a beta reading group? Congratulate yourself! You've put yourself out there!

Did you read one of the recommended books I mentioned in this guide? Great! Pat yourself on the back! Get up and do a Snoopy dance because you're that much more informed...and by a respected, talented, and bestselling author, no doubt.

Did you make it to the gym twice a week every week this month like you planned? Excellent! Your brain and body will be ever grateful that you've nurtured them with the power of exercise. Celebrate by treating yourself to a new workout shirt or download a new song for your next treadmill session. (Do not be that person that celebrates with a decadent treat. You're not a dog.)

Wrote an article for your blog about the latest book you read? Perfect! Tell your most supportive friend or loved one how happy you are to be contributing to a world of readers that shares the same passions as you.

The point is, don't live your life giving all your focus to the work, to the hardships, to the failures. Celebrate the wins, every little one, and you'll feel your faith and confidence in yourself increase little by little.

My final bit of advice to you, dear friend, is to have fun. I've covered a lot of ground in this book, and I know it can feel overwhelming, but really it just takes a bit of practice. If you truly love to read, love the idea of being a part of the creative process, then beta reading is an excellent skill to learn. It's so much fun. And you never know, maybe one day you'll find you want to take a stab at writing some fiction of your own. What better way to learn than this? (Combined, of course, with reading tons of great works already published.) The difference now is you've learned how to read with a purpose. So read voraciously. Read with a passion. Read with a purpose. Read to become Lit-Lucrative™. If nothing else, your life will be enriched with wonderful stories, valuable lessons, amazing histories, relationships with creative minds, and possibly the best hobby or career you ever could have dreamed of.

## PART III RECAP

In this section you have learned

- some helpful tips and lessons in etiquette for the professional beta reader
- what to expect from authors regarding your services
- of some handy-dandy templates to use for your services and as added value items to offer your authors
- a beta reader can work with the following tools:

PC OR DESKTOP WITH MS WORD (TRACK CHANGES)
TABLET WITH AN ANNOTATION APP
NOTEBOOK
PEN/PENCIL/HIGHLIGHTER/STICKY NOTES (IF READING HARD COPY)

- of some additional resources that may help you on your beta reading journey
- some steps to take to build confidence with this super fun skill set
- some helpful tips to stay focused and build confidence

## PART III RECOMMENDED READING

*You Are a Badass®: How to Stop Doubting Your Greatness and Start Living an Awesome Life* by Jen Sincero

I recommend *You Are a Badass* for those who feel mired by self-doubt and self-sabotaging beliefs that keep you from getting what you want out of life. Learning new skills is fun; putting them into action can be a bit scary. Because Ms. Sincero is such a funny and inspiring writer, I thought this would be an enlightening and fun read to give you that kick in the pants you need to unleash yourself into this new part of the literary world! And don't worry. If you're afraid it will be one of those boring self-help woo-woo books, fear not. Sincero's a real hoot.

# ABOUT THE AUTHOR

"I always come to life after coming to books"

— Jorge Luis Borges

I'm Dedrie and I've created Lit-Lucrative™—a budding e-school created to teach and embolden those wanting to enrich their lives with the wonderful world of books—to help fuel a passion I have for literature and the art of writing and reading with a purpose. This passion of mine started at an early age. At seven years old, I was interviewed on a stage (I was a pageant brat in the South) and asked what I wanted to be when I grew up. My response: a writer and a tap dancer. Lofty!

I do both. I do not earn any income from tap dancing (goals!), but I certainly love it. And I did not always earn an income writing or working with words. In fact, once I hit the age where I needed to get serious about the "What do you want to be?" question, I was of the mind that I could not do what I loved *and* merit a reasonable living doing it. Somewhere along the way I became stifled in my ambitions. So I just chose a fine-enough career and went for it.

For almost two decades I worked in healthcare in some capacity or another and enjoyed parts of it. But I felt stuck. It certainly didn't feel like I was doing anything I was passionate about—I had the typical American work week/work year where I busted my butt all year for a measly week or two of vacation, only to return knowing I wouldn't be able to do it again for another year. I had an overall sense of unfulfillment and felt mired in a passionless job. So I took some time to evaluate my life.

I contemplated all that I love and what my perfect life would look like, had I the choice. I considered my happiness, my goals, my physical health, my emotional health, and my financial health. I considered the balance, or lack thereof, in my life, observing the teetering of work and rest, work and play, and its constant battle to sink me. Fulfilling activities that surfaced over and over were reading and writing and traveling. *Does reading and writing make me happy? Yes. Does it contribute to my overall sense of well-being? Yes. How does it affect my financial health? Well, other than frequent trips to the bookstore denting my pocketbook, I don't know. Hmm.* This gave me something to meditate on. And meditate, I did.

I decided that I wanted to somehow earn a living in the literary world and be able to do so from anywhere I chose. But how? A career in the literary field felt foreign and beyond reach. And what were the options even? I had an education, but it was in healthcare.

I deduced that I obviously had to start all over. And at thirty-something, I did. I went back to college and enrolled in the English and Creative Writing (with a focus in fiction) program at Southern New Hampshire University. I also enrolled in every online editorial, publishing, writing, business development, and marketing course I could afford (aka charge to a credit card). Let me tell you, I've been one busy girl!

While working full-time, going to school for creative writing, taking online courses in editing, copyediting, proofreading, business creation and development, and authorpreneurship, I decided to start an editorial business. In addition, I read countless books, listened to numerous podcasts, sat through way too many webinars, and searched through hundreds of blogs and online articles to gain as much knowledge as possible. I attended as many author events as possible, learning firsthand what successful (even award-winning) published authors find crucial to their success. (Beta readers are high on the list!)

I cannot tell you how much knowledge I've scooped up over the past years just researching this. But what I **can** tell you is that much of what I spent time on could have easily been condensed. I would have loved to have found a course (that wasn't years of time and tuition…arm and a leg) or book that was that one-stop shop when it came to getting all my ducks in a row for a career in this field. And I had the hardest time finding any resources specifically for beta reading. So I decided to create one just for you!

At the time of this writing, I am still attending university. I can't help it; I love it! I am still educating myself as much as possible in the art of writing. I am still reading, reading, reading. But I've decided that I would feel absolutely giddy and honored to be able to share all I have learned with you and what has worked for me in my business. I would love nothing more than for you to read this book, love it, learn from it, earn from it, and then shout to the world that you have a new skill set that you love and can do anytime, anywhere.

And so that is my mission. I do not guarantee that beta reading is for everyone, but I do know that striving to learn something new or to improve in any way can do nothing but good for the soul. I love that I get to do something I love and am rewarded for it. My wish is the same for you.

Fellow book lover, it was a pleasure to introduce myself to you. I certainly hope you find this book valuable and love beta reading as much as I do!

# NOTES

The thing I struggled with most having a 9-5 job was the dreaded time-off requests. Something about having to ask permission to spend time with my friends and family never settled with me. I had a decent job working in healthcare—I love to help others—but what I love more is freedom (and freedom opens doors to many ways to help folks). The companies I worked for would (almost) always approve the requests, but it came with the knowledge that I'd have to make up those patient visits when I returned. Not really much of a holiday.

The most precious thing working with authors (and writing my own books) has given me is freedom. I work hard—not that it feels like work—but it's on my terms. And I haven't had to submit a time-off request to my *new* boss...well, ever.

If getting rich is what you're after, let me be candid—you're not gonna get monetarily rich with beta reading. You *can* earn while you read. So if a supplemental income would help out, go for it. Become a beta reader and be that subtle voice that helps an author become a best seller. Want even more ways to earn while reading? Consider copyediting, proofreading, book formatting, cover designing—there's so many ways. You absolutely can earn a living with one or two editorial skill sets.

As a beta, more than anything you'll be enriched by the work itself. If ever I was stranded on an island with only one wish, it would be to have all the books. Books enrich our lives unlike anything else on Earth. They are food for the soul, the mind, the heart. Love can be found lingering between the lines; a mystery can hide in the shadows beneath the cover; an adventure can race you from one page to the next. I just think it's pretty cool to be a part of the success of a book. If you'd like to learn even more about the fascinating skill of beta reading, check out *How to Become a Successful Beta Reader Book 2: Mastering the Art of Crafting Feedback*. I think you'll love it.

## ADDITIONAL RESOURCES

∼

IF YOU'D LIKE MORE HELP IN YOUR JOURNEY TO BECOMING A SUCCESSFUL BETA READER, THE FOLLOWING RESOURCES ARE AVAILABLE TO YOU:

*How to Become a Successful Beta Reader Book 2: Mastering the Art of Crafting Feedback* will go deeper into the act of linking reader opinions to the fundamentals of fiction and the art of crafting those opinions into feedback authors will value.

Click HERE for *Book 2* or find it at DedrieMarie.com/beta-reader-book-2.

Want to learn how to use the skills you've learned and turn them into an author services business? *How to Become a Successful Beta Reader Book 3: Establishing Your Beta Reading Business* will show you how to establish, market, and grow you biz.

Click HERE for *Book 3* or find it at DedrieMarie.com/beta-reader-book-3.

Want a comprehensive step-by-step course to take you from scratch to established? BECOMING LIT-LUCRATIVE WITH BETA READING is a multi-media online course made for anyone looking to get their foot in the door as an author service provider starting with beta reading.

Enroll HERE for online courses or visit
www.DedrieMarie.com/lit-u.

**I share useful links and tips. Connect with me:**
(f) www.facebook.com/dedriereads
(p) www.pinterest.com/dedriemarie
(t) www.twitter.com/dedriemarie
(w) www.dedriemarie.com

MORE BOOKS AND COURSES BY DEDRIE MARIE:

**Fiction Books in Progress:** Southern Gothic Mystery (written under Bebo Franklin)
*Elemdale Book 1*
*Elemdale Book 2*
*Elemdale Book 3*
You can sign up to be notified of new releases, giveaways, and pre-release specials—plus get a free short story from Bebo Franklin!

**Courses:**
COMMA SUTRA: Proofreading Fiction

## LEAVE A REVIEW

∽

Also, my new book junkie friend, I'd love to get your feedback on this book—positive or negative. My aim is to share the knowledge I've gained. I think it's our duty as fellow humans. But I don't claim to be an expert, just a lover of the craft.

If you have any comments or questions about the information here, shoot me an email at lit-lucrative@dedriemarie.com. I'd love to hear from you.

And of course, don't forget to **leave a review**—again, good or bad. Reviews help others make an informed decision about taking a chance on a book. You can leave reviews on Goodreads and Amazon.

Thank you for the courtesy of reading this book. I hope you've found it helpful in some way.

Happy reading,
*Dedrie*

# THE OBLIGATORY DISCLAIMER

While every effort has been made to accurately represent how to identify and use the fundamentals of fiction to beta read for self-publishing authors for free, quid pro quo, or a fee, there is no guarantee that you will earn any money. Any person or product that tells you otherwise is lying—as nothing in life is guaranteed.

There are affiliate links within this book to products and services that I personally use and recommend. This means I receive a small percentage of sales with no extra cost to you; and in some cases, you may receive a discount for using my links. I only recommend services that I personally use and believe are great for doing this work! If you're wondering why I recommend author services for you, the beta reader, it's because at some point your author will ask for advice. Wouldn't it be great if you could point them in the right direction? Going above and beyond to help your clients is THE BEST way to keep them and maybe get a few word-of-mouth referrals from them. It's a win-win.

**FREE VIDEO TRAINING**
Get the system I use to make my reading habit work for me:
www.DedrieMarie.com/start-beta-reading
Hope to see you there!
*Dedrie Marie*

www.ingramcontent.com/pod-product-compliance
Lightning Source LLC
Chambersburg PA
CBHW070928030426
42336CB00014BA/2582